C000180279

SUNLIGHT AND SHADOWS

WRITERS IN THE SOUTH OF FRANCE

JULIA CARTER

First published in 2021 by Julia Carter

Copyright © Julia Carter 2021

The moral right of Julia Carter to be identified as the
author of this work has been asserted in accordance
with the Copyright, Designs and Patents Act 1988.

All rights reserved. No part of this publication may be
reproduced or transmitted in any form or by any means,
electronic or mechanical including photocopying, recording
or any information storage or retrieval system, without
prior permission in writing from the publishers.

Every effort has been made to contact copyright holders.
However, the publisher will be glad to rectify in future editions
any inadvertent omissions brought to their attention.

Plate section photographs courtesy of:
National Library of New Zealand • Alamy • Topfoto
Shutterstock • Mary Evans Picture Library • Bridgeman Images
AKG-images • National Portrait Library

ISBN 978-1-913532-05-5

Also available as an ebook
ISBN 978-1-913532-06-2

Typeset by seagulls.net
Cover design by Kid-ethic
Project management by whitefox
Printed and bound by CPI Group (UK) Ltd, Croydon, CR0 4YY

To Pat for everything

All along the coast from Huxley Point and Castle Wharton to Cape Maugham, little colonies of angry giants had settled themselves…

Cyril Connolly, *The Rock Pool*

PROLOGUE

In the south-east corner of France, tucked between the mountains of the Alpes-Maritimes and the sea, is a narrow strip of
rather pebbly, inundated coastline with the most romantic reputation in the world.

The French Riviera was the name given to this sheltered
strip of coastline between Italy and Cannes, bathed by the calm
seas of the Mediterranean and protected from the icy winds of
the north. While the rest of Europe suffered snow and fog in
winter, here were trees hung with ripening oranges and lemons,
and flowers bloomed. In the nineteenth century, the leisured
aristocracy established the Nice social season on the Riviera for
two to three months after Christmas every year. It was a congenial mix of familiar and foreign as Russian, German, British and
Belgian aristocrats, emperors and monarchs mingled on the
shores of the Mediterranean. King Leopold of the Belgians
bought up a deserted promontory at Cap Ferrat and established
a hunting estate, chasing wild boar and deer among the pine
forests; the British prime minister Lord Salisbury built a house

overlooking the sea at Beaulieu and rode his tricycle brought from England, while Queen Victoria and her party took over floors in one of the grand hotels opening in Nice, Grasse and Menton. Regularly visiting her prime minister in Beaulieu, the Queen grew familiar with the road from Nice and noticed a frequent traveller: a poor man with a dog cart. Taking pity on the dog, the Queen had a water trough for dogs erected at a particularly steep part of the journey and it still stands there today. All along the coast a string of villas sprang up, settings for lavish balls and parties – the famed Parc de Valrose had a theatre for 400, and others had beautifully landscaped parks in which guests could walk beneath wisteria-hung pergolas and marvel at collections of plants brought from all over the world. When the orange harvest failed in Nice and the community faced poverty, it was the English winter residents who commissioned the building of a promenade to create work in the area and it is still, today, named La Promenade des Anglais. 'Anglais' can also be found in the names of apartment blocks and streets throughout the Riviera as the wealth of those original English visitors left its mark.

Gradually, with the coming of the railway, the pattern of visitors changed, and the exclusivity of the resort diminished slightly as more people could afford the trip. Hotels, rather than private villas, were the new destinations of choice and these sprang up all along the coast, vying with each other to offer bathrooms and ballrooms and all the luxury of the late Victorian and early Edwardian periods. Every morning, fleets of carriages would drive the guests down the road into town and along the sea. In the evenings they would drop them at the many nightclubs and restaurants that were now springing up along the main roads in Nice and Cannes, for this was the Belle Époque – the period at the turn of the nineteenth and twentieth centuries when the Côte d'Azur was in its first heyday and when its name was coined.

It was the Americans who, after the First World War, discovered the potential of the French Mediterranean as a summer resort. Accustomed as they were to the heat of the US, the young Americans who swarmed to Paris looked for somewhere warmer than Normandy for the summer and when an adventurous couple, the Murphys, persuaded an Antibes hotel to try out opening one floor for the summer, it became a huge success. The sunshine, the swimming and the beauty of Juan-les-Pins and Antibes brought Picasso and Mistinguett, Hemingway and Chanel, Dos Passos and Cole Porter to the summer Riviera. It was a young and experimental season, contrasting with the formality of the traditional winter set.

Meanwhile, something else was afoot: as artists moved out of their studios and into the open air, painters were discovering the rare quality of the light in the south – Cézanne (himself from Provence), Van Gogh and Renoir came south and marvelled in the colours they found there. They were joined by the Fauves, experimenting with colour, and then later by the Cubists and the greatest names of the early twentieth century – Picasso, Matisse, Dufy and Chagall – who settled along the coast around Nice.

In turn, they brought other creative spirits: photographers and cinema directors, dancers and writers.

It is above all the artists whose works created our image of the Riviera, in those paintings we all know so well of wide blue seas and decorated windowsills. Whenever I come to Nice, I experience a sense of déjà vu. Staring, jaw dropped, at the sweep of the deep-blue Baie des Anges, flecked by boats and fringed by palm trees, I feel surprisingly at home and connected. This is a view I have known in paintings and reproductions all my life: it hung on my adolescent walls in posters and decorated my bookshelves in cards. The works of Dufy, Matisse and Picasso have made the scenery more familiar than the view from my window. And in greeting the scene, I am perhaps also greeting the ghost of my younger self.

Yet, oddly, I am still unprepared for the beauty of the views down from the Grande Corniche, the high road at the top of the hills, and the vistas that open around the bends that snake along the sides of the hills, revealing breathtaking glimpses of bays far, far below and, nearer to hand, expanses of wild lavender and thyme – all dominated by the 'perched' villages, effortlessly clinging to a hilltop castle, aged and serene.

This is paradise, a combination of natural and man-made beauty unrivalled anywhere else in the world, and yet there is always something that checks me, despite – or perhaps because of – the beauty. Is it the knowledge that such a paradise must also have its own serpent? Is it a fear that there is something strangely transient in this moment of beauty, which cannot last, or is it the sense of corruption in the glittering crowds, the gleaming yachts and the sleek limos that gather outside the smart restaurants? Somerset Maugham said of neighbouring Monte Carlo that it was: 'A sunny place for shady people.'

It was in an attempt to discover the roots of my unease that I turned to the works of the writers who had lived on the Riviera. Since the painters had recreated its image so vividly, I assumed the writers would help me to understand it through their writing. Of the many authors who lived or stayed on the Côte d'Azur I chose six, who all wrote there in the period between the wars when the social scene of the Riviera was at its height. I imagined them meeting for a glass of rosé under the evening plane trees of a village square to read their work in progress and to discuss news from London's literary scene. I wondered what they thought of each other and what the relationships had involved in terms of affairs. Above all, I wanted to discover what they wrote about this corner of the French coast where they had made their temporary home.

I was disappointed. Although the writers had all come to the Riviera to write, they did not write about the Riviera. Of them all, only Fitzgerald wrote a novel set in, and about, the South of France and its destructive effect on the marriage of his hero, Dick Diver. Maugham, who lived on Cap Ferrat for forty years, wrote only two short stories set there, and in those the setting is immaterial. Mansfield set only one of her short stories there and Wharton never alluded to the South of France, even though her novel *Summer* seems redolent of southern France in its imagery.

Huxley did not write anything set on the Riviera, and though Cocteau's early verse and his drawings and mosaics are filled with references to the area, its history and its people, his plays are never set there.

Nor did the writers cluster together to read and discuss their works. Though they often had mutual friends and acquaintances, they mostly avoided each other – in part out of a sense of competition, but in part too because their time was too precious. All had their own reasons for coming south but all shared at least one: the need for privacy in which to concentrate on writing, and this was so treasured they were unwilling to risk its loss through socialising. Only Maugham and Wharton, who lived permanently on the Côte d'Azur and had the means to employ staff to protect them, entertained formally, but often in order to be able to choose their companions.

There is a sadly amusing account of a fatal meeting between Wharton and Fitzgerald, which epitomises the problematic potential of socialising between writers. Both were eminent American authors living in France and they shared a high professional respect for each other's work. In every other way they were profoundly opposed: Wharton, much older than Fitzgerald, came from an old and aristocratic New York family and belonged to a society hermetically sealed against the advances of such as Fitzgerald or his creation, Gatsby. Fitzgerald, meanwhile, epitomised new New York: young, vibrant, the very term 'The Jazz Age' was coined by him with its flappers and bobbed hair, smoking and cocktails. When Wharton invited Fitzgerald to tea he was overwhelmed and, in typical fashion, resorted to Dutch courage. Arriving already drunk, he found Wharton's formal conversation and long silences embarrassing and felt the need to liven up the party in his usual way. Staggering drunkenly towards the fireplace, he proceeded to tell an unsuitable story of friends who had stayed a night in a Parisian brothel, mistaking it for a hotel. The story fell flat and, in the ensuing silence, Wharton asked the pertinent question: 'But what did they *do* in the bordello?'

In a journal entry for 5 July 1925, Wharton recorded the visit as a disaster.

Though not quite such flops, other social meetings between the writers were equally unproductive. Maugham, after entertaining Cocteau, remarked dryly: 'Of course M. Cocteau amuses his servants.'[1]

He found little common ground with Wharton. She, meanwhile, enjoyed the occasional company of the Huxleys, but found Cocteau's pretensions over modern art unbearable. Generally, the writers maintained their solitude and lived not in the South of France but in their imaginations.

It is this obvious but profound difference between them and the painters that explains the lack of novels and short stories set in the South of France. For the writers, their location was not directly important to their writing. They came for the peace and the relatively cheap cost of living and they stayed often because they fell in love with the beauty. They all produced their greatest work in the south: Mansfield's *Prelude*, Cocteau's

La Belle et la Bête, Wharton's *The Age of Innocence*, Fitzgerald's *Tender is the Night*, Maugham's *Cakes and Ale* and Huxley's *Brave New World* were all written in the South of France and are arguably their creators' masterpieces.

This book is an attempt to find out more about the writers who went to the South of France, their reasons for going and to see how the Riviera influenced them as writers. If painters of the South of France have coloured how we 'see' the landscape, what can these writers tell us about the Côte d'Azur and the way we see it today?

CONTENTS

KATHERINE MANSFIELD

Katherine Mansfield's short story 'Honeymoon', originally published in 1923 is the story of a newlywed couple taking afternoon tea in one of the Riviera cafés. The young wife is blissfully happy until she hears an unexpected note of sadness in the music being played by the band. All at once she has an insight into something deeper and more difficult to grasp.

> There are people like this. There is suffering. And she looked
> at that gorgeous sea, lapping the land as though it loved it,
> and the sky, bright with the brightness before evening. Had
> she and George the right to be so happy?[2]

For Mansfield, the beauty of France was intermingled with the terror she had known there – the themes of her life were the coexistence of beauty and suffering, of happiness and pain, and ultimately of life and death. In 'Honeymoon', she used all her skill to convey, in a typically underplayed moment, every-thing she had learned in the South of France.

Mansfield had come to France originally to forget the war and to find a way to write again. As her train clattered through the changing landscapes, she caught sight of the country stations with their huddles of silent soldiers. It was November 1915 and she was numb to everything around her, haunted by thoughts of the last moments of her younger brother, Leslie, killed on the battlefield of northern France. In her head, she replayed his last words, intended for her.

Lift my head, Katy, I can't breathe.

What was he thinking about as he struggled to get his last breath? Where did he think they were? Back home in New Zealand? In her house in London where he came on his last visit?

Do you remember, Katy?

Upstairs, in the house in Acacia Road in St John's Wood, they had been children again in New Zealand. Chummie and Katy Beauchamp, climbing the pear tree in Tinakori Road; clinging to each other on the wobbly garden seat in Karori. All Leslie's life she had been there, from that very first time she had seen him, a bundle in their grandmother's arms, and he had been simply 'Boy', the long-awaited son after so many girls. Later she had called him 'Chummie' because that was what he was, her faithful companion and intimate friend.

Lift my head, Katy, I can't breathe.

New Zealand was often in her dreams now. Sometimes they were sunny dreams of the long days of her childhood, and sometimes they were terrible nightmares in which she was grown up, living in London but on a visit to New Zealand. In those dreams she would lose her return ticket for England and she would wake up, drenched in sweat, in a panic that she was exiled for ever from London, where she had found her liberation and her success as a writer. She had created a new identity for herself in England, and even a new name: she was now Katherine Mansfield, a writer, partner of the literary critic Jack Middleton Murry and a member of the inner circle of artistic Londoners. She had come a long way from New Zealand.

Jack (John) Middleton Murry was asleep now, facing her in the rocking train compartment, his generous mouth slightly open and his square face tilted forward. On the table between them was a sheaf of manuscripts for his new magazine, *Signature*, and an article he was trying to write about their friend and partner, David (D.H.) Lawrence. Lawrence's latest novel, *The Rainbow* (1915), was causing a ridiculous scandal, which was threatening to undermine the future of *Signature* itself. Mansfield knew Murry wanted to talk about his worries, but she couldn't drag herself away from her own grieving, from hearing Chummie's last words:

God forgive me for all I have done.

The journey had been her idea; she had thought that travel might help to heal her grief and she had to get away from the house, which was now so full of painful memories of Leslie's last visit and their happy laughter in her study. In southern France, she had thought, she would begin to forget Leslie, and might even be able to try to write again. Instead, she felt worse – it was as though she was carrying Chummie with her, like some invisible ghost: everything she saw, she wanted to point out to him,

3

and if he could not share her experiences, they had no value to her; she might as well be blind. The world felt insubstantial, like a long, uneasy, watery ripple, flowing over a still pool where Leslie was lying.

They left the train in Marseilles and she arranged Leslie's photograph on the mantelpiece in their hotel bedroom. The city was seething with soldiers and sailors from across France and her lands beyond the sea; a mix of languages and uniforms crowded the streets and lined the quays, embarking and disembarking in a chaotic flow. Mansfield's head reeled from the noise and her eyes were dazzled by the light that turned everything bright and glittering, like exotic parrots' wings or flashy canna lilies. It was impossible to write in Marseilles.

Lift my head, Katy, I can't breathe.

In the quiet village of Cassis, along the coast, there were *pointus*, twin-pointed fishing boats, tied up below the towering calanque cliffs, as there had been since Roman times. Women in shawls walked down the narrow cobbled streets to the harbour to buy fish. Old men sat among the nets and peeling boats, smoking. Bright geraniums and cyclamen grew in pots outside the narrow houses and, high above the bay, the château fort, like a child's sandcastle, stood on its rocky outcrop pierced with southern cypresses, surrounded by olive trees, green with leaf.

In the sunny hotel room, Murry and Mansfield set out their papers. They would write here. But the next day the weather turned. Icy wind whistled under the ill-fitting door, lifting the thin rugs off the cold floor. The papers they had laid out so hopefully were scattered on the writing table. The hotel had no heating and Mansfield was smitten with a bad attack of her rheumatism and had to go to bed to get warm. Murry, miserable and sick from food poisoning, blamed the French. It grew worse. Low cloud obscured first the château and then the entire hillside, closing in on them as a grey veil covered the sea. Rainwater poured, like a drain, down the steep streets of the village and ended in a torrent that drowned the harbour steps and plunged into the sea.

Suddenly, as so often happened when things went wrong, Mansfield was overwhelmed by a violent hatred for Murry and wanted him out of her life. He was keen to get back to London and the editing of *Signature*, but he could not leave her in the cold hotel in Cassis. They moved east again, along the coast to Bandol, where Mansfield found the Beau Rivage, a small, comfortable hotel in the middle of the village where she felt she would be happy alone – she had to be alone, she insisted, if she wanted to write. From the hotel there were views over the front and back bays and a garden with seats where, on a sunny day, she could sit and watch the islands on the horizon. The air at Bandol smelt familiar – a blend of pine and sand, a childhood memory of the beach in New Zealand. The wind had dropped, the sea was blue, and a miraculous spring sun warmed her back as she walked along the beach. She loved being by the sea: smelling and hearing it felt like a homecoming and made her realise how much she had missed it all the time she had been away.

In the fields were huge drifts of pale yellow jonquils, their delicate scent promising better things to come; the water in the bay had turned hyacinth blue in the afternoon sunlight and, screwing up her eyes against the shimmer of the sea, she felt for the first time the beauty of the view. In her daily walks, Mansfield remembered the promise she had made to her brother on his last visit. She had promised him then that she would write about their happy childhood together, the magic of their homeland, for readers who had never been there to experience some of its beauty for themselves. It was a difficult task but, now, in Bandol, for the first time since his death, she began to feel as though she might, just, be able to do it. She felt energised and excited, as she had not been for months: writing the book would mean immersing herself in those precious memories of Chummie, which would help to keep him alive, both for her and for the readers of the story. In her imagination she could see the book published and its dedication inscribed on the title page, *Dedicated to the memory of Leslie Heron Beauchamp.*

At home there had been long, hot, motionless middays on the beach, when the tide flopped lazily against the empty sand and her feet burned when she went out to play, forgetting her sandshoes, set out to dry on the bungalow windowsill. Sometimes she preferred to stay indoors, lying in her underwear in the cool of her grandmother's bedroom, watching her knitting in her rocking chair, while they talked about dead uncles and how everyone has to die, even Chummie and Katy. In the South of France the sunlight seemed to spin like a silver coin dropped into the rock pools, and rosemary grew in tufts between the red rocks. The days merged into each other and into the remembered days of her childhood. From her hotel room she watched the long evenings when the sun seemed unwilling to dip below the horizon, turning the sky a pink-yellow like unripe cherries, and the stiff silhouettes of palm trees, like children's cut-outs, stood out, black, against an unreal, canary-yellow sky. She felt like a child again, tired out and happy after a day on the beach, her cheeks sunburned, as she went home to bed, dreaming of the smell of the gum trees and the feel of sand between her toes.

Mansfield's contentment came not only from the beauty of her new surroundings in the Mediterranean climate, but because she found herself writing again, and well. Her story about their childhood was bringing New Zealand to life, in all its shimmering radiance, just as she wanted it to. It would feel like the moment just after the sun has set and the sky is still bright, for Chummie had been her sun and now he was gone and all that remained was an afterglow that struggled to illuminate her world.

* * *

The First World War had destroyed life as it had been, for ever. No one could forget the horror of war, and nor should they. For Mansfield and her contemporaries, the deaths and injuries of so many friends, lovers and relations was matched by the breakdown of civilisation, the end of society as they had known it. From now on, she and everyone else had to live with the knowledge that everything they valued, everything that had made life worth living and celebrating, was destroyed and lost. There was no going back and, if you were honest, no way of pretending it had not happened.

Mansfield could never write in the old pre-war manner. She needed to find a new way of writing, a new voice, that would reflect this dramatically changed world. The task she had set herself was difficult and, in her struggles, she regretted sending Middleton Murry away; he understood her quest and would be a useful and supportive companion. Murry was in London working on the journal he edited, writing his book on Shakespeare, meeting his friends – writers she sometimes despised and sometimes admired. Forgetting her earlier irritation with Murry, she now longed for them to be reunited and, in this loving mood, she made a significant discovery.

It was a small villa, stone-built and strangely elegant, set back from the coast road with its own garden and a veranda. There was a little round table and bench where she could imagine the two of them writing every day, a living room with a fireplace, and a cosy double bedroom with shuttered windows looking out to sea. Mansfield in her letters begged Murry to come and, when he agreed, she rushed to rent the Villa Pauline, which she scrubbed and polished for his arrival, even dashing to the market early in the morning to buy baskets of violets and roses to fill the house with perfume.

Miraculously, the reality of their life together lived up to her romantic expectations. The Villa Pauline suited them both, their relationship was in an easy, harmonious phase and their happiness translated into successful writing. Every day they sat at their stone table while the mimosa came into yellow flower in the woods behind the house and, in the corner of the garden, the almond tree burst into pale pink bud. Murry worked hard, immersed in his study of Shakespeare, while Mansfield, trying to find her new voice, thought of Chummie, of their house in New Zealand by the sea, of her schooldays in London, where she and her sisters had all attended Queen's College in Harley Street.

Then one day, quite by chance, she found among her papers a manuscript she had written earlier. It was an unfinished short story, called 'The Aloe', the name of that exotic Mediterranean plant that throws up a huge yellow flower out of its clump of razor-sharp leaves. The story was set in New Zealand but inspired by the South of France and, rereading it now, she suddenly realised what she had been trying to write. This was the story of Leslie's birth, of Boy, as he was called when he was a baby, coming into her world one hot summer's day, when nothing moved, a white bundle in her grandmother's arms; a big head, still as a doll, as he lay on a rug in the long grass under the tree in the garden. The story she was looking for and the voice she was trying to find to bring the mysteries of New Zealand into full-blown life had suddenly materialised in 'The Aloe' and she set to writing it again, full of the excitement of her discovery. 'The Aloe' turned into *Prelude* (1918), the longest piece she had written so far and written in her new style, which managed so successfully to merge inner consciousness with external observation. Even Mansfield, who frequently doubted her own work, knew that she had written something exceptional and allowed herself to feel pleased with it.

Life could not get much better. Those spring days, writing with Murry in their garden, and the evenings, reading companionably by the fire, were simple and intensely happy. It seemed to Mansfield that she had, at last, mastered the art of happiness, that skill that had so often eluded her and, now that she had found it, she was determined never to lose again.

In late spring they set off, full of hope, for England. Mansfield was buoyed up by the knowledge of her achievement, the success of her relationship with Murry and, perhaps as a result, the improvement in her health. But they moved to Cornwall, where they rented an unheated cottage near D.H. Lawrence and his wife, Frieda. It was a miserable time of cold, wet weather, which brought on rheumatism for Mansfield, and extreme tiredness that left her unable to write. Relations between Mansfield and Murry deteriorated again and those between the two couples collapsed even more violently. Although she had always been fond of Lawrence, Mansfield was shocked at how he had changed since she had last seen him. Now she found him argumentative, especially with Frieda, a German aristocrat, who could be equally argumentative back, though she was not his physical equal, and when Lawrence physically attacked her, Mansfield was drawn into the confrontation as Frieda sheltered with her. Murry and Lawrence had a long-standing and complex relationship that involved homoeroticism, although both men refused to have a sexual relationship, becoming blood brothers in a romantic German fashion to signify their union. In Cornwall they took long walks together, leaving the invalid Mansfield to the care of Frieda. However, Lawrence's relationship with Mansfield was equally complicated. In his highly successful novel *Women in Love* (1920), he explores his fascination with Mansfield and Murry through the characters Gerald Crich and Gudrun Brangwen. Gudrun is an independent woman and an artist, who defies social conventions by openly living with her lover in an apparently highly destructive relationship. The novel included a homoerotic, naked wrestling match between Rupert Birkin (Lawrence) and Gerald Crich (Murry), while his knowledge of Mansfield's inner life is exposed in his description of Gudrun and is, incidentally, one with which Mansfield would not have disagreed.

> Did she want 'goodness'? Who but a fool would accept this of Gudrun? This was but the street view of her wants. Cross the threshold, and you found her completely, completely, cynical about the social world and its advantages. Once inside the house of her soul and there was a pungent atmosphere of corrosion ... and a vivid, subtle, critical consciousness, that saw the world distorted, horrific.[3]

Given the tense interplay of attraction and jealousy, it was inevitable that relations between the couples broke down and also that Mansfield characteristically plotted her own, independent escape by inviting herself to visit the aristocratic socialite Lady Ottoline Morrell, who was a friend of both Lawrence and Murry.

11

Mansfield had never met her hostess before but seized her chance to flee, leaving Murry to sort things out with the Lawrences.

By autumn, Mansfield and Murry were together in London, where the Woolfs were about to publish *Prelude* at their Hogarth Press. It was a triumph for Mansfield, but all was not going well. She was suffering from a cough and shortness of breath and feared she might have consumption. She went to see a consumption specialist, who confirmed her fears – she had a shadow on the lung, a precursor of TB. Gazing through the window at the Virginia creeper, already turning red, she realised that life would go on as normal, regardless of her health. Fiddling with his notes, the specialist asked her if she had children.

There had been the bundle in the pension in Germany, the miscarriage of her pregnancy with Garnet Trowell, but nothing since. The signs had been there again, and she had a bank account for the baby, but then it too went away.

She shook her head. 'No.'

But what would he have said if I had told him that until a few days ago I had had a little child, aged five and three quarters – of undetermined sex. Some days it was a boy. For two years now it had very often been a girl.

Journal, December 1919

The doctor's smooth voice rolled on: 'advise no sexual intimacy … stay in a sanatorium … or, at the least, spend the winter in the sun.'

Mansfield's mind flashed back to 1908, when she was living with the Trowells, a family she knew from New Zealand, whom she had met again in London. She and Garnet Trowell became lovers while his parents were away, and when they came home they threw her out of the house. She was pregnant. Garnet, a musician, could not keep her and a baby, but she knew someone who could. That was George, dependable George Bowden, who was eleven years older than her and an established choirmaster. He had helped her find work teaching elocution and voice projection to would-be vicars. Now he agreed to marry her, to provide respectability for the baby. But she could not bear to live with him and fled London on her wedding day to join Garnet on tour in the north of England.

Thousands of miles away, Mansfield's mother saw the notice of her daughter's marriage that Bowden had placed in *The Times*. Boarding the next boat to England, she accosted her daughter, now five months pregnant, and took charge. Mansfield was taken to a hotel in a small German spa where she was to stay until the baby arrived. Her mother sailed back to New Zealand for another daughter's wedding.

Mansfield quickly moved out of the hotel and into a guest house, or pension, which was the setting for her first volume of published short stories, *In a German Pension* (1911). Two important things happened to her while she was there: first, she miscarried the baby and coped with it alone. Second, she met and fell in love with a Polish poet and writer staying at the spa. Floryan Sobieniowski introduced Mansfield to Eastern

Europe and Russian writing. He was probably also the man who gave her incurable gonorrhoea, which made her infertile and contributed to her early death. Claire Tomalin, in her biography of Mansfield, makes this assertion based upon the typical side effects from which Mansfield suffered, including rheumatism, chronic breathing problems and heart conditions.[4]

TB, even without gonorrhoea, was at that time nearly always fatal. The conventional solution, with a rare chance of a cure, was to spend time in a specialist clinic in the mountains, resting and breathing clean air. Such sanatoria were to Mansfield 'warehouses for the dying'. For her, writing came first, and she knew it would be impossible to write in such an artificial atmosphere. Unwilling to sacrifice any of the months remaining to her, she turned her back on the suggestion of a sanatorium, but grasped eagerly at the chance to be somewhere warm in the winter. 'Some time in the warmth might, just might, do the trick,' she heard the doctor say. 'In any case, a damp, cold winter in London would not be the thing, not the thing at all.'

She had a memory of sparkling sea and green pines and she smelled the scent of jonquils in the warm air. She felt herself flooded with hope again. She would go back to the South of France and spring into leaf and flower and be able to write.

It was 1916 and France was at war. Although she and Murry were reconciled, he could not travel with her, and her loyal school friend, Ida, was involved with war work. So Mansfield travelled alone. The trains were full of soldiers, some with hideous wounds, coming or going to the Front. There were no timetables and tedious delays, no food and hardly anywhere to sit. Mansfield struggled with the red-hot iron inside her lung, which was burning right through her. At Marseilles, where she went to the buffet to get a meal, she was ordered away from the table by a fellow diner, repulsed by her sick appearance. When the train finally crawled into Bandol station, she was too weak to move; a group of Serbian officers lifted her off the train and onto the deserted platform. She was alone, cold and weary. Her trunk was lost, the hotel had clearly not received her telegram and was not expecting her, and her head was ringing with the terrible tales of consumption that her civilian travelling companions had been telling each other, perhaps in the belief that poor Mansfield did not understand them. Exhausted and grateful for the bed that was eventually found for her, she crept into it with brandy and a hot water bottle and was determined to stay there until the weather – or her health – improved.

The next morning, lying in bed with her shutters wide open to frame the view, Mansfield watched the sun rising over the landscape, silhouetting the palm trees and racing across the hyacinth-blue bay to turn the hills from violet to jade. She stayed in bed until lunchtime to recover from the journey. Lying in such luxury, looking out on such a wonderful sight, she told Murry in a letter:

> I'll tell you exactly what I feel like. I feel like a fly who has been dropped in a milk-jug and fished out again, but is still

15

too milky and drowned to start cleaning up yet. Letters will take a long time – perhaps 6 or 8 days – so do not worry if you do not hear from me.

Letter to Murry, 11 January 1918

But two days later she wrote that she had walked to look at the villa they had rented the year before. It was a painful journey, physically demanding in her state of health and emotionally draining. The route was poignant with happy memories, which affected her badly:

When I came to the vineyard where the two little boys used to work I realised quite suddenly that I was suffering – terribly, terribly, and was quite faint with this emotion.

Letter to Murry, 18 January 1918

She went on along the path until she reached the Villa Pauline where she and Murry had been so happy.

I thought I had never, in my happiest memories, realised all its beauty.

(ibid.)

Madame did not recognise her at first, she was so changed by her illness, but when she did, she welcomed her into the villa, which she was airing.

We sat on either side of the table, she in your place, I with my back to the fire in mine, and had a long talk.

(ibid.)

The landlady wanted news of Middleton Murry and spoke with warmth of their stay the previous year. She told Mansfield about the price of meat and the shortage of bread and Mansfield:

…felt that somewhere upstairs, you and I lay like the little Babes in the Tower, smothered under pillows … When I saw my photograph, that you had left on the wall, I nearly broke down, and finally I came away and leaned a long time on the wall at the bottom of our little road … As I came down your beautiful narrow steps, it began to rain. Big soft reluctant drops fell on my hands and face. The light was flashing through the dusk from the lighthouse, and a swarm of black soldiers was kicking something about on the sand among the palm-trees – a dead dog perhaps, or a little tied-up kitten.

(ibid.)

By early February, spring had come to Bandol and Mansfield was absorbed in her short story 'Je ne parle pas français'. Aware of the natural beauty around her, she was also rejoicing in her inner life and the acute pleasure she derived from writing.

I've two 'kick offs' in the writing game. One is joy – real joy – the thing that made me write when we lived at Pauline, and that sort of writing I could only do in just that state of being in some blissful way *at peace*. ... The other 'kick off' is my original one, and (had I not known love) it would have been my all. ... an extremely deep sense of hopelessness, of everything doomed to disaster, almost wilfully, stupidly ... There! As I took out a cigarette paper I got it exactly – *a cry against corruption* ... and I mean corruption in its widest sense of course.

Letter to Murry, 3 February 1918

In 'Je ne parle pas français', she expressed her feelings of loss, isolation and loneliness. The story is about a naive young Englishwoman who elopes to Paris with her English lover. Once there, he deserts her, leaving her alone in a strange city where she does not speak the language and knows only one person, an old friend of the lover's, a French gigolo who is moved by her situation but is unable to reach out to help her. Given Mansfield's own circumstances, alone, ill and not communicating her real feelings to anyone, it is easy to see the inspiration for the story (she even gives the woman her own nickname, 'Mouse'). Similarly, both the men are aspects of Murry – his passivity, his indecisiveness and ultimately, she felt, his lack of feeling for her. Indeed, the story is a thinly veiled and cleverly constructed attack on Murry, including details of an affair he had had before he met Mansfield. Although she appears to be projecting herself as the dependent 'Mouse', that is disingenuous: Mansfield was no mouse and had chosen to separate herself from Murry by coming to France. Nevertheless, the emotions she expressed were doubtless those she genuinely felt at that moment. Murry was seriously upset by the story:

> …it upset me – I'm an awful child.
>
> Letter from Murry to Mansfield, 15 February 1918

He wrote to her and then praised her writing but still did not come to her side. Now on her own in Bandol, fighting for time to write, the nights were not easy. Racked by the growing pain in her lung, she was plagued by her fears and terrible panics. As the house shook in the winter gales, she felt as though she were adrift in a boat. She dreamed of the Ancient Mariner and thought about the wives of the poor fishermen out at sea and of Shelley, the drowned poet. Death was all around her at night, like a huge, black carrion crow overhead or a pack of howling dogs encircling her, waiting to pounce. Her only escape was reading, and she lit her candle and devoured books as fast as Murry could send them, reading volumes of Dickens and contemporary novels to review for the new journal he edited, *The Athenaeum.*

She thought of Keats, the poet with TB who knew he was dying and doubted that his own work would outlive him: *Here lies one whose name was writ in water.* Keats understood.

> Here, where men sit and hear each other groan
> Where palsy shakes a few, sad, last grey hairs…[5]

19

And then one morning, as she sprang out of bed to fling her shutters open to the bright day, she tasted something dark and salty in her mouth.

> It was bright red blood. ... Oh, yes, of course I am frightened. But for two reasons only. I don't want to be ill, I mean 'seriously', away from Jack. Jack is the first thought. 2nd I don't want to find this is real consumption, perhaps it's going to gallop ... and I shan't have my work written. *That's what matters.* How unbearable it would be to die, leave 'scraps', 'bits', nothing real finished.
>
> Journal, 1918

She waited until later in the afternoon to write to Murry. By that time she had composed herself and had found a voice in which to break the news. It was the brittle, artificially bright tone of the nursery, as though he was not her lover but her son, whom she had to protect.

> This is *not* serious, does not keep me in bed, is absolutely easily curable...
>
> Letter to Murry, 19 February 1918

In effect, she constructed a controlling wall of lies and silence around her fatal illness that made it impossible for Murry ever to talk to her frankly about her fears and her death. Perhaps this was the only way she could cope with her terrible knowledge and it was a useful tactic to help her make the most of the short time left to her. On the other hand, it made it impossible for her and Murry to confide in each other and reduced their relationship at a time when she most needed its intimacy. Later, she blamed Murry for his lack of sympathy and care, and it was true that he took a long time to realise just how grave her situation was – but it was never entirely his fault. Mansfield had her own share of responsibility and blame.

Mansfield's letter to Murry crossed with one to her, in which he wrote:

> Your letters are wonderful, like yellow flowers, narcissus, that have grown up in the night. They scent me with love.
>
> Letter from Murry to Mansfield, 21 February 1918

The letter ends:

> All our dreams will come true, my precious heart, cross my own heart, straight dinkum I believe utterly…
>
> (ibid.)

In the immediate aftermath of her letter telling him of her illness, Murry took her at her word. She had told him not to come out to see her and he respected that command but sensitive friends, like Virginia Woolf, realised how worried he was (Woolf Diary, 17 March 1918) and how hard he was working to procure her papers to travel home. There was some good news too: Mansfield's long-awaited divorce from her marriage of convenience to George Bowden had come through at last and she and Murry were planning to marry in London on her return. Meanwhile, Ida Baker, Mansfield's old school friend, travelled across war-torn France to nurse her. Ida was Mansfield's opposite, a slow, reliable, thoroughly practical, hard-working woman – in all ways but one, a very 'ordinary' person. Yet her devotion to Mansfield, and the fact that she had recognised Mansfield's special qualities when they were still at school, suggest that there was more to Ida Baker than Mansfield realised. Bad at Ida's sort of devotion and resenting her own dependency, she found Ida irritating and her conversation boring. Seeing that her friend wanted to nurse her, she churlishly rebelled and, ignoring the rigours of the journey Ida had been through for her sake, announced her intention to go home immediately. The war meant constant delays obtaining travel permits, doctor's visits and stops while they queued for papers, and in Paris they were forced to wait for days, giving Mansfield her first experience of the reality of the war. She was horrified by the sight of the bomb-blown houses, their pitiful rooms exposed to passers-by, their contents hanging scattered on trees. She hated the noise of the guns and the airless shelters where unwashed Parisians were forced to take refuge. Though she admired the French tenacity of spirit in the face of so much destruction, she was shocked at their apparent acceptance of bestial terror and the grotesque insensitivity that let them find humour even at the mouth of the grave.

In her own highly charged state, France became a Sodom and Gomorrah and she set her face firmly towards the cliffs of Dover, where she would throw off the nightmare scenes of France and join her lover in marriage and a new, peaceful life.

Mansfield married Murry in May 1918 in Kensington Registry Office. It was a small and quiet affair with the bride so thin her ring fell off her finger, and her dress did little to hide her skeletal frame. Mansfield tried to hide the signs of illness in her face and grew her fringe long, but this only accentuated the pallor of her skin and made her eyes stand out like black coals glowering reproachfully in her emaciated face. Their married home was in Hampstead, where Murry's hopes that the altitude might help Mansfield's chest were soon dashed. Increasingly forced to live as an invalid, she kept indoors, in her bed or easy chair, and depended on visitors like D.H. Lawrence and Virginia Woolf to keep her abreast with things. She was still busy reviewing books for *The Athenaeum* when her doctor advised her, once again, to avoid an English winter.

Mansfield's memories of war-torn France were so terrible that she decided not to return there. Instead, she, Ida and Murry set off for Italy, planning a stay in the smart Italian Riviera resort of San Remo, just across the border from France. En route they visited Mansfield's cousin Connie, who spent her winters in Menton, where she lived with a friend in a comfortable villa. Arriving in San Remo in early September, they were met by the soft warmth of an Indian summer. Roses and plumbago continued to flower, bright cascades of flowers dripped

23

from the trees and, in the beds, bees hummed around lavender and begonias. In the villa gardens there were date palms
and citrus trees, and by the entrance to their hotel a proud
aloe was in full flower, butter-yellow, erect, towering above the
flowers in the bed. However, they were not welcome at the hotel.
San Remo was a commercial resort and the hotel managers
were not happy to admit a guest who was so clearly ill with an
incurable infection. Instead, they moved into a small house in
Ospedaletti. The 'casetta', as Mansfield immediately christened
it, was basic but conveniently isolated and ideal for an invalid.
Murry stayed just long enough to see his wife and Ida settled in
and then left for London and *The Athenaeum*, promising to keep
Mansfield supplied with books to read and review.

The casetta was charming as long as the sun shone; a house
for lovers, Mansfield called it, thinking romantically of Murry
and watching the swallows in the evenings, swooping low over
the sea. Determined to make the most of her time in the beloved
southern sun, she sat outside in the garden perched above the
sea, feeling deliciously detached from the world, as though she
were on a sailing boat surrounded by the sparkling ocean. In
the daily journal she was keeping, for publication, she brought
to life the minutiae of the insects and flowers in the garden and
recorded her occasional slow walks in the olive groves behind the
house, where little had changed since classical times. Her journal
described her few visitors – the Italian gardener and his wife,
and the woman who did the laundry. It was a limited but still
wonderful existence, and on 14 October, her thirty-first birthday,

24

she recorded with real pleasure the new daisies she had found growing among the gravel and the flights of tiny yellow butterflies she had seen fluttering across the beds. She had survived the year and she felt, genuinely, that she had a lot to celebrate.

But there were other days when she was too ill to stir from her chair and the world narrowed to streams of silver sunlight on an empty sea, sprinkled with the dots of distant sailing boats, like black spots on the lung. On those bad days, she railed against the meagreness of her existence and raged at the lack of congenial company and intellectual stimulation. She vented her frustration on poor Ida, lashing out against her friend's limitations and physical appearance and demonising her into a wardress keeping Mansfield a prisoner. Her violent hatred grew with her helplessness and despair. She had fantasies in which she revelled in killing Ida and disposing of the body; she found it impossible to look at her companion, and meals became a torture to her. Her only escape was her reviewing, and she threw herself into this task with an energy that bordered on the manic. She wrote cruel and cutting reviews and, in her frequent letters to Murry, criticised other contributors to the magazine viciously. Nor did she limit her criticism to others: she was also harsh on herself, desperately begging Murry for reassurance about her piece on Dostoyevsky, anxiously asking him if she had missed the point in Virginia Woolf.

With November came dark clouds that rolled in off the sea, and lashing gales. The casetta, perched on its clifftop, was cold, unheated and without water, which Ida had to bring up, daily, from a well. Isolated and fragile, the walls shook as the wind blew and with every gust it felt as though the roof was going to come off. At night, as she listened to the crash of the waves pounding the cliff, Mansfield wondered if the house could withstand the force of sea and wind. Weak and defenceless, her little home grew to symbolise her own condition, surrounded, she felt, by death, which was waiting for a chance to break through her frail defences and swoop her away. Unable to write and in despair, Mansfield felt that Murry had deserted her. Though unfair, her little poem of 4 December 1919 reads like one of Wordsworth's *Lyrical Ballads* and is just as moving.

The New Husband
Someone came to me and said
Forget, forget that you've been wed.
Who's your man to leave you be
Ill and cold in a far country?
Who's the husband – who's the stone
Could leave a child like you alone?

Letter to Murry, 4 December 1919

Her condition worsened so that she now spent the days in bed and in her journal she recorded an enormous and radical inner change. She described a vivid dream in which her whole body broke into pieces like glass amid…

…a low confused din. … When I woke up I thought there had been a violent earthquake. But all was still. It slowly

26

dawned upon me – the conviction that in that dream I died. I shall go on living now – it may be for months, or for weeks or days or hours. Time is not. In that dream I died.

Journal, 15 December 1919

At her lowest point, her small world was transformed by a visit from her father and her cousin Connie. Horrified by the cold and discomfort of the casetta and shocked at Mansfield's emaciated appearance, Connie Beauchamp insisted she move into a nursing home in Menton and then to her comfortable villa. For months Mansfield had resisted her invitations, but now, suffering from rheumatism and exhausted with despair, she gave in and in the New Year of 1920 she moved across the border and back to France. The nursing home was like a taste of heaven. Sunshine poured through the four huge windows of her bedroom, showing up the vases of flowers and the generous writing desk, complete with inkwell and stack of new paper, and from outside came the sounds of birdsong and gardeners working in the immaculate grounds. Breakfast was brought by a maid so pretty she looked as though she had stepped out of an opera, and, most wonderful of all, on the tray with her tea there was hot buttered toast with honey, which she ate sitting up against a great bank of pillows, in her comfortable bed.

Like the flower she had once likened herself to, she slowly recovered, throwing off the tortured madness of those last weeks in Ospedaletti and becoming herself again. She took slow walks along the raked gravel paths in the garden down to the heated gazebo, from where she could see the blue of the sea, framed between fronds of stiff palms and dark green pines. The garden was filled with the heady scent of orange blossom and early roses were blooming in the shelter of the wall, along which a dark-eyed orange creeper hung like a carpet. Once again, she felt grateful to be alive.

She discharged herself from the nursing home and took up her room in Connie's comfortable villa in Garavan, the eastern-most part of Menton, close up against the border with Italy but with a climate so different it felt as though they were hundreds of miles apart. A long favourite of the British, the town boasted, at the time of Mansfield's visit, a firm of English lawyers, doctors, a library and a church. There were English tea rooms and English gardens and, above all, English fellow-minded trav-ellers with whom one could talk or play bridge. The winds that had pounded the beach at Ospedaletti did not blow here, where the dramatic snow-capped mountains shielded the town.

Mansfield loved the pretty villa set in its lush gardens and the wide, quiet streets of the suburb of Garavan. She enjoyed the motor car drives they went on, out of the town and away from the sea into the rural hinterland of steep valleys covered in dark pine trees and dotted with red-roofed stone cottages. The harvests of tomatoes and grapes were spread out to dry in the winter sun, while in the valley bottom the farm-ers slowly trimmed their vines and burned their clippings on bonfires, whose columns of white smoke rose in the golden air, like stone pillars.

As she grew stronger, Mansfield could manage leisurely walks along the promenade or in the pretty town with its picturesque church and elaborate fountain dedicated to Queen Victoria. There were well-kept parks, bright with exotic flowers and tea rooms and cafés where Connie would meet her friends while the waves broke in the sunshine outside and a chamber orchestra played. Ida, who had been placed in a pension while Mansfield stayed in the big house, came to join them on their walks before going back to England again to look after her father.

After the social isolation of the casetta, Mansfield was thrilled to be meeting people again and found many of her cousin's friends agreeable and interesting. One couple in particular became her own especial friends. The Schiffs were a literary couple from London who had a delightful house just outside the 'perched' village of Roquebrune, overlooking the sea. Both Violet and Sydney had read Mansfield's stories and were as thrilled to meet her as she was to find them. In their Provençal garden, with its lavender and lemon trees, they argued the relative merits of English, European and Russian novelists against a background of rushing water and croaking frogs.

In her latest story, 'The Man Without a Temperament' (1920), an English couple are forced to live in a Mediterranean hotel on account of the wife's illness. But it is the husband who is the focus of the short story, which explores the impact of living in 'paradise' with its emptiness and idleness. The story bravely explores the reality of facing up to death and the corrosive influence it has on those around it. The landscape is that of the coast and hinterland of Menton or Ospedaletti. The aloe, which features in this story too, is now a frothy, gaudy spike of overblown flowers, showy, corrupt and dying…

> Every leaf, every flower in the garden lay open, motionless, as if exhausted, and a sweet, rich, rank smell filled the quivering air.[6]

…while the modest valley behind the coast has an unassuming, quiet beauty of tumble-down peasants' houses, where tomatoes are drying outside:

> The late sunlight, deep, golden, lay in the cup of the valley; there was a smell of charcoal in the air. In the gardens the men were cutting grapes. He watched a man standing in the greenish shade, raising up, holding a black cluster in one hand, taking the knife from his belt, cutting, laying the bunch in a flat boat-shaped basket. The man worked leisurely, silently, taking hundreds of years over the job.[7]

By May, restored by her time in the sun, she went back to London. She had forgotten how gloomy the city could be. To her Mediterranean eye, everything was grey and covered in a thin film of dust. Writing to her friends the Schiffs, she described the scene at Murry's office:

> …a smell of stone and dust.

Everyone she met seemed timorous and without vitality, as though prematurely old. Even the so-called luminaries of the literary scene, like Aldous Huxley – whom she described as 'wavering like a candle' – and E.M. Forster, struck her as depressed and pessimistic; other colleagues of Murry's were 'poor silly old men harking back to the mud in Flanders' (letter to Sydney and Violet Schiff, 4 May 1920).

Murry was involved with work and Mansfield's health was not improving. As soon as she could, she set off again with faithful Ida, for what was to be her last visit to the Riviera. This time they took a villa from Connie Beauchamp. The Isola Bella was a small villa, close by the large house but with its own garden, veranda and a studio where Mansfield could work undisturbed. The house and the studio are still there today, squeezed in behind the coastal railway line on its descent into Italy, and with luminous views of the empty sea, which turns silver and gold, depending on the time of day.

Mansfield's publishers, Methuen, had commissioned two books by spring, and there was another being published by Constable. She was more determined than ever to write a novel with the time left to her, in her beloved South of France. Everything she looked at was imbued with a painterly magic, as vivid as something from a picture book – the great piles of green and orange gourds and pumpkins piled along the edges of fields; the red tomatoes, spread out to dry outside the little houses; old men working in their shirt-sleeves and a dark-skinned boy leading his high-stepping goat across a field fringed with green poplars and red willows against a bright sky. Even the ripe figs she ate for breakfast tasted so much better than their 'soprano' northern cousins.

Mansfield's heady state, her heightened awareness of the beauty around her and even her joyfulness signalled her approaching death. Her journal recorded the moments of almost sublime intensity when the ordinary world was transformed. She captured the childish ecstasy of an autumn thunderstorm in a letter to Murry on 19 September 1920:

> The drops of rain were as big as marguerite daisies ... the sky was all glittering with broken light – the sun a huge splash of silver. The drops were like silver *fishes* hanging from the trees. I drank the rain from the peach leaves...

In the garden there were hours of pleasure just watching and marvelling at the creatures and then describing them to Murry in her letters: there were young wasps fighting over a tiny leaf, a lizard devouring an ant with a flick of its terrible tongue, frogs, mice and even a snake, which she describes erotically:

> Now there's an asp come out of its hole – a slender creature, red, about 12 inches long. It lies moving its quick head ... I'll catch this one for you at the risk of my life and put it in your Shakespeare for a marker ... You will have to hold your Shakespeare very *firmly* to prevent it wriggling, Anthony darling.
>
> Lovingly yours
>
> Egypt

> Letter to Murry, 10 October 1920

32

She didn't stop writing. Between 1920 and 1921, in her little garden studio, surrounded by green oaks and mimosa trees, she finished 'The Man Without a Temperament' and wrote 'The Young Girl', 'Poison', 'Miss Brill', 'Life of Ma Parker' and 'The Daughters of the Late Colonel'. She was also reading books to review in *The Athenaeum* and reading for herself. In her current overwrought state, her critical feelings were sharp and she returned to her theme of the modern novel and its failure to adapt to post-war consciousness. Although she had so little time, she was determined to find that new voice that reflected and fitted the new world. In *Prelude* she had mastered what she called 'continuity' (we might call it 'consciousness'); now she managed it again in 'At the Bay'. This burst of creative energy, exceptional in a healthy person and extraordinary in Mansfield's state of illness, was, she felt, in large part due to the light and climate of the South of France, where she felt herself come to life. She wrote:

> My light goes out in England, or it's a very small and miserable *shiner*.

Letter to Murry, 28 October 1928

Once again she had vivid dreams and there is a note of manic optimism in her letters, which probably hides her deeper feelings. She could no longer keep up her journal entries as they forced her to contemplate the truth, from which she sought to escape through her fiction. In October 1920 she told Murry about her bad days and then apologised for burdening him. The letter was disingenuous at best and deliberately dismissive of Murry's feelings for her at worst:

> *Whatever* my feelings are, I am not justified in giving way to
> them before you.
>
> Letter to Murry, 4 October 1920

Yet later in the month she wrote triumphantly:

> I confronted myself.

And she emerged in:

> ...a different state of being to any I have ever known and if
> I were to sin now it would be 'mortal'.
>
> Letter to Murry, 31 October 1920

Whether it was the letter that persuaded him how little time
there was left, or whether he wanted to escape from *The
Athenaeum*, which was not going well, Murry decided to be with
Mansfield permanently. He came to Menton for Christmas and
found her very much declined. She now spent most of the day
in bed. When their lease on the villa was up, the Murrys and
faithful Ida decided to try the healing air of the Alps and moved
to Montana (Crans-Montana nowadays).

Here, Mansfield wrote avidly, finishing at least five works
while in great physical distress. It was here that she wrote the
haunting short story 'Honeymoon', which juxtaposes the beauty
of the Riviera with the sadness of human life, as heard in the
strains of a piece of music played by the band. It was Mansfield's

farewell to her beloved South of France and her realisation that the beauty of nature and the sadness of life can coexist.

This sadness, an awareness of what Mansfield called 'corruption', is an essential part of existence. Though it had once threatened to take over her world and render it dark and ugly, she had arrived at a knowledge that allowed her, and perhaps her readers, to see it could flourish side by side with all the love and beauty and sunlight of the world.

Mansfield never returned to the South of France, but her little studio is still there. To reach it, you turn off the main road onto rue Mansfield and follow that past prosperous suburban villas, then turn off and take a country track under the railway line until you are almost in Italy. There on the left is a little garden house: Mansfield's studio, in which she enjoyed a huge creative surge and lived in a state of near ecstasy. A tattered sign tells you there is a museum, but it is never open. Probably it, too, would smell of stone and memories of old wars, but Mansfield's legacy was one of creative triumph over physical destruction and, standing in the quiet lane, I remember her for the courage that forced her to recognise that both are equally part of the human condition. Mansfield was a liberated woman long before her time and she paid a heavy price for her freedoms. But she achieved great wisdom towards the end of her tragically short life and realised that beauty was not cancelled out by corruption of the body. Disease, destructive as it is, cannot obliterate beauty and happiness.

JEAN COCTEAU

In the small port of Villefranche, just beyond Nice, sits a statue of Jean Cocteau engraved with his line 'When I look at Villefranche, I see my youth'. The greatest all-round French artist of the 1920s, Jean Cocteau was a very active member of Parisian society, yet he spent every summer in a modest quayside hotel in the village of Villefranche-sur-Mer. The Hôtel Welcome hosted a unique mix of French sailors, bohemian artists and prostitutes from Marseilles presided over by their madame. Here, Cocteau worked on poetry, ballets and oratorios with fellow residents and neighbours – Stravinsky, Picasso, Chanel, Diaghilev and Isadora Duncan. For a short while, between the two world wars, everyone in his sphere who was creative and fashionable seemed to be living, writing, composing, dancing and designing in the South of France. Cocteau came south to find consolation after the death of his lover and then to continue the romance he developed with the village, where he could escape the demands of Paris and indulge in the beauty of the setting, greatly enhanced by the opium to which he was addicted.

Jean Cocteau was born just outside Paris and grew up in an upper-middle-class family, which, after his father's suicide, included his grandparents as well as his brother and mother. It was a sheltered and privileged childhood in the centre of old Paris, but young Cocteau did not enjoy school and in fact failed his bacca-lauréat. Nonetheless, he began to show outstanding promise as a poet and as a social mixer. Openly gay, he was good-looking and attractive to established writers like Proust (who modelled his character Octave in *À la Recherche du Temps Perdu* (1913) on him) and to less established but influential figures like Édouard de Max, a leading actor who appeared on stage opposite Sarah Bernhardt. De Max was so taken with Cocteau that he arranged for him to give a reading of his first collection of poems at a Paris theatre, and the success of the event brought him invitations and introductions everywhere in Parisian artistic circles, at the age of nineteen. He met the Russian émigrés – Diaghilev, Nijinsky and Bakst – and went to the first production of the Ballets Russes, which took Paris by storm, eventually persuading Diaghilev to give him a job, designing a poster for his next production.

The American writer Edith Wharton remembers meeting him with André Gide at the home of the artist Jacques-Émile Blanche, who introduced her to much of the Parisian literary and artistic society. Cocteau struck her as a golden boy,

> a young man of nineteen or twenty, who at that time vibrated with all the youth of the world, a passionately imaginative youth to whom every great line of poetry was a sunrise,

every sunset the foundation of the Heavenly City ... I have known no other young man who so recalled Wordsworth's 'Bliss was it in that dawn to be alive'. Every subject touched on – and in his company they were countless – was lit up by his young enthusiasm.[8]

In 1913 Cocteau began a friendship with Stravinsky, whose composition *Le Sacre du Printemps* (1913) had been received by the Parisian first-night audience with boos and a riot. This excited Cocteau, who had a strong desire to shock and provoke his audiences, and he switched the focus of his energies from Diaghilev to Stravinsky. The outbreak of the First World War brought this life to a temporary halt: Cocteau's modernist novel *Le Potomak* (1919), inspired by Stravinsky, was already with the publisher when war was declared and the world of literature stopped.

When he returned from the war, in which he served as a private ambulance attendant, with a uniform specially designed for him, Cocteau's friendships expanded again: he worked closely with Erik Satie, another modernist musician and leader of the group Les Six, all of whom became part of his coterie, bringing jazz and Latin music into cabaret society. Picasso encouraged him in his drawing and through him he got to know the other important modern painters: Braque, Gris and Modigliani. Inspired by the excitement of so many new ideas, Cocteau persuaded Picasso and Satie to work with him on a modern ballet to be produced by Diaghilev. *Parade* (1913) was a new form of ballet with modern music, cubist set and costume design, and the use of mime and mirrors to daring effect. As well as surprising and even shocking the audience, the ballet also raised serious questions on industrialisation and capitalism. Reviewed by Apollinaire, it was hailed as the future: '...[it] cannot fail to tempt the elect or radically change the arts and customs of humanity'.[9]

Cocteau became an icon for French youth: students hung photographs of him on their walls; others wrote him letters enclosing their own poetry; and many flocked to his apartment in the rue d'Anjou (shared with his mother), where his levee (formal getting up in the morning, surrounded by admirers) was attended by his young fans. One of these was Raymond Radiguet, a schoolboy poet with whom Cocteau fell in love.

In a relationship that was part lover, part father and son and part tutor and gifted pupil, the two lived together from 1919 to Radiguet's death in 1923. Radiguet was himself a gifted writer and his first novel won an international prize and was praised by Aldous Huxley when it was translated into English. Together they enjoyed the artistic and cultural life of Paris: on 3 May, Radiguet was invited to give an address at the Collège de France; on 15 May he was awarded the Prix du Nouveau Monde for his first novel, *Le Diable au Corps* (1923). Later in the month he and Cocteau wore elaborate fancy dress for the annual ball given by the Comte and Comtesse de Beaumont; in June, Cocteau's ballet *Les Mariés de la Tour Eiffel* (1921) was performed by a visiting Swedish company, and Clive Bell (a prominent member of the Bloomsbury set and brother-in-law of Virginia Woolf) spent the evening with them at Le Boeuf sur le Toit, a cabaret bar named after a work of Cocteau's and a second home for Les Six and other members of Cocteau's coterie, who gathered there nightly. They were at the premiere of Stravinsky's *Les Noces* (1947) and then went to a riverboat party for the composer; in July there was Milhaud's house-warming party and frequent picnics in the park; in August they went to the sea with friends.

It was there, on the Atlantic coast near Arcachon, that Radiguet first became ill, possibly after eating an oyster. His condition worsened gradually throughout the summer, but he was still working on his second novel. He and Cocteau moved on to the Mediterranean and eventually back to Paris, where Cocteau asked his friend Coco Chanel for help. She found him the best doctor and hospital in Paris (and paid the bills), but Radiguet died of typhoid. Cocteau was too devastated to attend the funeral.

His immediate response was 'to run away'. First to Monte Carlo, where he joined the Ballets Russes, and then to Villefranche, where his friend the composer Georges Auric invited him to share rented rooms for the summer of 1924. In the Villa le Calme, a pension overlooking the port at Villefranche, Cocteau enjoyed the sight of the soldiers from the Chasseurs Alpins regiment, who had their barracks there.

Today, Villefranche is a quiet fishing village, surrounded by the intensely coloured waters of its deep bay. When Cocteau arrived, the busy port was packed with sailors in the bars along the narrow streets and locals milling on the quay. Cocteau wrote to Valentine and Jean Hugo, 'I am suffering – suffering in the sun, and this is atrocious' (7 August 1924), and to the writer Gide,

'Here I am trying to live, or, rather, I am trying to teach the death within me how to live. It is all hideously painful' (August 1924).

Although he wrote cheerfully to his mother of trips to Nice, boat journeys and exciting car rides, he admitted to his friends that they all left him deeply depressed. To help him cope with the pain, Cocteau began taking opium. He had already experimented with it during his stay in Monte Carlo and he now began to indulge heavily. He described vividly the effect of his smoking.

Sleep was my refuge. The prospect of waking kept me from sleeping properly and determined my dreams. In the morning I could no longer face resuming life. Reality and dream overlapped, making an unsightly blob. I got up, shaved, dressed with people in my room and let myself be dragged anywhere. Oh, those mornings! It was like being thrown back into dirty water and made to swim. In this state one cannot bear to read a newspaper: such evidence of general activity and those who wrote about it is murderous. My flight into opium is Freud's 'flight into sickness' – waves of sweat, chills, yawns, running nose, choking fits, a lump in the solar plexus. I confess that at the time I didn't realise the cause of those symptoms.

Letter to Marcel Jouhandeau, summer 1924

* * *

By this time, Cocteau had moved into a room at the Hôtel Welcome. Here, he would sit for days at a time in a drug-induced semi-stupor, looking at himself in the mirror, drawing self-portraits and trying to answer the questions: Who am I? What am I? Gradually, the sketches became lighter and more humorous, decorated with notes and lines of poetry. They were published as a collection of thirty drawings with the title *Le Mystère de Jean l'Oiseleur* (John, the Bird Catcher) (1923), a reference to his own name, which contains the word 'cock', and its punning secondary meaning in both languages.

Emerging into daylight from the darkness of mourning, Cocteau began to appreciate the strange haven he had found at the Welcome, with its bohemian mix of guests and sailors.

> I'm living in a weird place. It's a box suspended in the upper branches of a flaming Christmas tree. On the first floor of this hotel-bordello sailors beat one another up and perform belly dances. I hear the base drum throbbing jazz; it's as if they were printing a paper in the basement.
>
> Letter to Marcel Jouhandeau[10]

He was to spend much of his time between 1924 and 1929 at the Hôtel Welcome. Images of mirrors, reflections and dreams, which recur as central themes and figures in his work throughout his life, began here, in his hotel room above the sunlit bay, in an opium-induced daze.

Earlier, when he and Radiguet were at Le Lavandou, further along the coast, Cocteau had written a poem, 'Jeu Royal', in which he describes the ordinary seaside hotel where they are staying in terms he could have used for the Welcome. This love poem also shows Cocteau's ability to bring together the classical and the contemporary, inspired by the Mediterranean.

Cheap hotel in front of the Mediterranean,
The morgue of dead sailors where Venus was born[11]

Living by the Mediterranean seemed to excite a return to classical literature as a way of understanding modern life. Cocteau returned to a work begun earlier, a modern play based on the story of Orpheus, called *Orphée* (1926) (later in his life, Cocteau turned his play into the well-known film). The play explores the two themes that occupied all of Cocteau's work – the death of a lover and the nature of the artist. In the classical story they are combined when Orpheus' love, Eurydice, dies and he rescues her from the underworld through his skill as a musician. Orphée moves between life and death by walking through a mirror, which represents the boundary between the two worlds. The image was derived from Cocteau's own journey to the underworld of his grief-induced drugged state, viewed in the mirror of his hotel room. Cocteau returned to Paris when the play opened there in 1926. It was an overnight success, and he was confirmed as the leading playwright of his generation.

Heading back down to Villefranche the next summer, flushed with his recent success, Cocteau, with his unerring instinct for time and place, had stumbled into this pretty fishing village at just the right time. The Hôtel Welcome was now home to a sprinkling of American writers and an eccentric medium, Lady

Rose, a British aristocrat, and her son, Francis, whom Cocteau
introduced to sex.

> The Hôtel Welcome became an international focal point,
> a *point de repère*, drawing Diaghilevians from Monte Carlo,
> Anglo-American millionaire bohemia from Nice, stray
> French counts, and consorts from all about. Behind its
> pink façade and *trompe l'œuil* shutters lay all the ingredients
> of an Alexandrian potpourri. The hotel formed part of a
> world half-drowned in its own fantasies. A world had been
> exploded by World War I and the *disjecta membra* of the wreck
> washed up all along the Riviera, like elegant fixtures of some
> luxury liner.[12]

Against a backdrop of the sailors and prostitutes, life at Hôtel
Welcome saw guests wandering in and out of each other's
rooms to read, recite and perform for one another. For Francis
Rose's seventeenth birthday, the hotel guests threw him a fancy-
dress party. His mother came with a Captain Williams, who
was dressed as a Basque peasant and accompanied by a donkey.
Isadora Duncan wore a diaphanous Greek tunic and brought
a troupe of young male dancers, who decorated the birthday
boy in flowers. There was a priest in purple socks, Cocteau's
friend Maurice Sachs in a Spanish-style clerical hat and a Lady
MacCarthy from Monte Carlo in a frilly green frock that made
her look like a cabbage. There was a hilarious fight when the
Captain threw his silver watch at Isadora Duncan, who was

embracing Francis Rose, and tore her tunic; she responded by flinging a mayonnaise-covered lobster into Lady MacCarthy's lap and a fight ensued between the American and Scots sailors.

Isadora Duncan had by now established a studio in a shack beyond the Promenade des Anglais in Nice. Further down the coast, at Antibes, the Fitzgeralds, Murphys, Hemingways and Picasso, Cocteau's great friend, could be found on the beach at La Garoupe, and at Mont Boron, the headland between Nice and Villefranche, Stravinsky, who worked with Cocteau on his ballet *Parade*, had a house.

At the end of that memorable summer, Cocteau stayed on in Villefranche to write the libretto for another classically inspired piece, *Oedipus Rex* (1925), in collaboration with Stravinsky. Intended as a surprise gift for Diaghilev, *Oedipus Rex* had a difficult gestation. Although the Russian composer had asked Cocteau to collaborate on the oratorio, he had not worked alone with him before. Now working with him daily (and well into the night), he told friends that he was irritated by his companion's manner, which he found affected and theatrical. He was perhaps being unfair: Cocteau was genuinely excited to be working with the great man and found his innovative music intoxicating. Walking back from the Mont Boron house, after a day spent working, Cocteau described his exhausted elation, '[his] ears still dazzled by the golden, anular, chiselled music of Oedipus Rex'[13] and his eye caught by the beauty of the bay of Villefranche, its night sky dissected by the beams from the Cap Ferrat lighthouse.

Yet although Stravinsky had commissioned him to compose a French libretto, which would be translated into Latin and sung, Cocteau had ideas of his own and to this end had fashioned a French spoken text to be narrated by himself as a one-man chorus. In the event, Diaghilev was not at all pleased with the gift of *Oedipus Rex* (he claimed that he had never fancied his mother) and the choreographer refused to have the piece performed in anything more than an un-staged concert version, in which Cocteau was not even invited to play 'his part'. Nevertheless, he managed to salvage what he could from his collaboration and published his French libretto in 1928 as *Oedipus Roi*, with the byline *Villefranche-sur-Mer*.

If the theme of Oedipus was unsuitable for Diaghilev and his relationship with his mother, it was highly pertinent for Cocteau, who lived part of the year with his mother in Paris well into his forties and, when her influence began to wane, he found proxy mothers in the form of wealthy, capable women who supported him emotionally and financially. Coco Chanel was one of these surrogate mothers, who not only designed costumes for his productions (her costumes for *Orphée* introduced casual fashion to the world) and underwrote his ventures but also paid for his frequent cures and drug rehabilitations.

Another fairy godmother was Marie-Laure, Comtesse de Noailles. Marie-Laure and her husband were serious patrons of contemporary arts. They commissioned the highly controversial concrete villa in cubist style along the coast at Hyères with a swimming pool and gym and that newest of fashions, a cinema.

Each year, the Noailles commissioned a new film in honour of Marie-Laure's birthday. Here, guests including Jean Cocteau and André Gide watched the work of two unknown cinematographers – Buñuel and Dalí – in their sensational surrealist film *Le Chien Andalou* (1929), and Cocteau was inspired by the potential of the new medium to write and direct *Le Sang d'un Poète* (*The Blood of the Poet*) (1932), which won critical acclaim, its familiar theme – a journey into the inner world of the poet – this time using the exciting techniques of cinematography to brilliant effect, cutting and superimposing images, in a 'surrealist' style.

Cocteau fell in love with the possibilities of film. It was the medium of the moment and it wasn't long before he had become one of its most successful exponents. Socially, too, the film world brought him into contact with good-looking young men and women – the actors who appeared in his works and the designers and artists who worked on them. The actor Jean Marais was his lover for many years. During the 1930s and again after the Second World War, Cocteau continued to make films and chase funding. It was through film that he met his last great benefactor and mother figure, who was to remain at his side for a decade: the young and newly married Francine Weisweiller. They met in 1950 when Cocteau was making *Les Enfants Terribles*, starring Francine's cousin Nicole de Rothschild. Cocteau was in his early sixties (but still slim and good-looking) and Francine was in her thirties. According to John Richardson, Picasso's biographer, Madame Weisweiller was an 'exquisitely dressed, excessively spoiled little beauty', who appointed herself as Cocteau's muse. Cocteau in turn became 'the man who came to dinner': he accepted an invitation to stay at Villa Santo Sospir on Cap Ferrat, and remained a more or less permanent fixture for the next decade. Francine was extremely rich in her own right as well as through her husband, Alec, an American millionaire; she was elegant and attractive and moved in the very best Parisian circles. Already an ardent supporter of Yves Saint Laurent, who dressed her for free, she persuaded her husband to invest in Cocteau's film and allowed some of it to be filmed in their palatial apartment on the Place des États-Unis.

Although by now Cocteau had bought himself a country retreat outside Paris, in Milly-la-Forêt, he was always keen to return to Villefranche and so he accepted his new friend's invitations to stay at her villa on Cap Ferrat. He repaid his benefactor's generosity by decorating the villa with paintings and mosaics. His rooms overlooked the sea, a place for his lover, Édouard Dermit, to work and space to entertain visitors. Here *Le Testament d'Orphée* (1960) was filmed and here, too, Cocteau entertained neighbours like Somerset Maugham and the Ali Khan or took the Weisweiller yacht, *Orphée II*, across to Saint-Tropez to have drinks with Picasso. It was while he was staying at the Villa Santo Sospir that Cocteau painted the chapel at Villefranche and the museum and town hall at Menton. Here, his drawings are playful but they lack the lightness and tenderness of his earlier work and seem to me formulaic rather than witty. He was now an old man, still seeking to recapture the golden days of his youth, when he could shock the world.

As the century moved on, so did taste and fashion, and Cocteau found his vast network of contacts and friends were no longer of such value or celebrity. One day, Francine Weisweiller told him he had overstayed his welcome at the Villa Santo Sospir. He retreated to his own villa at Milly-la-Forêt and was still writing when he suffered a heart attack. Although he recovered, he was shocked to be woken on the morning of 11 October 1963 by a Paris radio station and told of the death, in the early hours, of Édith Piaf. Cocteau turned down the invitation to join a memorial broadcast about her, saying he had had a bad night, which he now realised was caused by her death. At 1 p.m. he died of a heart attack.

Although he died in his house at Milly-la-Forêt, he is not forgotten in Villefranche. His rather unflattering statue stands on the quay opposite the Hôtel Welcome and the chapel he decorated for the fishermen still attracts regular visitors, who pay their entrance fee willingly for a glimpse of the interior. On the Cap, where he stayed with Francine Weisweiller so many times, the lane that runs past the Villa Santo Sospir is now called after him. I often park there when I am walking on the Cap in the cool of the evening. At the end of the Avenue Jean Cocteau, there is an electricity substation labelled *Cocteau. Danger de Mort*. He would have liked the joke.

EDITH WHARTON

Like so many writers of her generation, Edith Wharton was drawn to the classical associations of the South of France. Where Picasso and Cocteau had captured the classical history in their drawings of nymphs and satyrs, for writers such as Wharton, educated in the classical traditions, these were the foundations of culture and learning. Recovering from the destruction of civilisation in the wake of the First World War, there was comfort to be gained by being so close to this older, longer-lasting culture. 'One is beset by classical allusions, analogies of the golden age', she wrote in a journal.

Born into the very heights of New York society during the Civil War, Wharton first came to Hyères in 1915 to visit her friends, the French novelist Paul Bourget and his wife, Minnie, who had a holiday house there. Although she had never liked the fleshpots of Monaco and Cannes, she fell for the unspoiled area around Hyères. She stayed for a month. After the horrors of the First World War that she was experiencing in Paris:

It is delicious just to dawdle about in the sun, & smell the
eucalyptus & pines, & arrange bushels of flowers bought for
50 centimes under a yellow awning in a market smelling of
tunny fish & olives.

Letter to Elizabeth Cameron, 26 November 1915

When she returned after the war, in 1919, it was to claim for
herself a part of the paradise she found there to help her over-
come the trauma of the war and to acquire a villa in Hyères.

Wharton was in the process of establishing herself with a
life in France and so bought not one but two houses: one on
the outskirts of Paris for her summers and the other in Hyères,
near Toulon, for winter gardening and Christmas entertaining.
Making the decision to settle in France had been a long time
evolving for Wharton, who had spent much of the previous
decades trying to decide whether she belonged in the States
of her birth or the Europe of her adoption. The war and the
suffering she had witnessed and shared had made it clear that her
loyalties were now with the Europeans, especially the French, and
her acquisition of her two villas underlined this commitment.

Equally important was the fact that this was the first time
she had invested in owning her own home(s) since she and her
husband, Teddy Wharton, had created The Mount at the beginning of the century.

It had not been a happy marriage: Teddy Wharton was fifteen
years older than his twenty-three-year-old bride, and whereas
she had already co-authored a serious work on architectural

51

history, *The Decoration of Houses* (1897), Teddy had few intellectual interests. In 1901 the Whartons started work on The Mount, a hugely exciting and expensive country house, modelled on the English Belton House. It was a fitting project for the author of *The Decoration of Houses* and also a statement about their marriage and joint venture together. Lenox, Massachusetts, where the house was situated, was Wharton country and home to Teddy's mother. Teddy loved country pursuits and was keen to manage the small farm and business side of the estate as well as enjoying the hunting and fishing that went with the position. Edith Wharton threw herself into the design of the buildings and the park and gardens.

It was a vast undertaking that included a stable block and lodge house and 130 acres of landscaped grounds. There were Italianate gardens set on a sloping hillside, with splendid vistas between marble pillars of (designed) meadows, lake and woods. Wharton was a plantswoman as well as a designer and landscaper, and she relished the English country garden flowers she planted in their hundreds, for their delicate scent and colour, as much as she enjoyed walking the gravel paths to admire a view she had artfully constructed.

The house brought her the contentment to write fiction: her first novel, *The Valley of Decision* (1902), was written while she was working on the house and her second, the bestselling *The House of Mirth* (1905), was written at The Mount when it was completed.

The Mount suited Wharton; it allowed her time to write and to manage her social life – she was no longer living in a social setting like New York or Newport, Rhode Island, with irritating expectations, and could choose the friends she wanted to see by inviting them to stay. The house was designed in her imagination for gatherings of interesting and like-minded friends to gather on the terrace overlooking the gardens and to talk over dinner in the dining room and then walk through to the drawing room, without breaking off their conversation.

Wharton was successfully – and fairly uniquely – cultivating her own circle of friends, just as she did her garden. Cultured, educated and articulate friends were gathering around her, mainly men but not exclusively so, and characteristically for Wharton there was an unusual mix of young and old. Her friends, chosen for their minds and interests rather than their family or past, were a statement of the independence she had established for herself and her rejection of her family's traditional values. Finally, for a woman who was essentially shy and singular, the setting allowed her to establish the lifestyle she wanted, away from the eyes of family or neighbours as she had endured previously in New York or Newport. Wharton was not rebellious and the life she wanted to lead would not strike us as noteworthy today, but in those days to crave independence and to strive to choose her own friends was unusual, and something to be fought for.

Her guest list was impressive: Henry James, the great Anglo-American novelist, came with his friend Howard Sturgis; Walter Berry, a lifelong friend, was always present; Robert Norton, an English civil servant and amateur artist of note; Robert Grant, a writer, and Bill Richardson, a lawyer; Edward Robinson, curator of the Metropolitan Museum in New York; Daisy and Winthrop

Chanler, who introduced Wharton to Roosevelt; Charles Eliot Norton, the Harvard academic, and his daughter Sally all came to stay in small groups and enjoyed Wharton's fine food and wine (though she herself did not drink).

Wharton organised a firm schedule for her guests: she wrote in bed in the mornings, so they could not expect to see her until 11 a.m., when they would set off for a picnic lunch (to save the staff work), followed by a walk or sightseeing tour. In the evenings there was talk: her guests were good conversationalists with intellectual and cultural interests, who could be depended on to have read the latest biographies or books of importance and could discuss them knowledgeably.

The Whartons had a routine of travel and divided the year between the States and Europe, partly to further her knowledge of Italian design and architecture; but, returning to Lenox from Italy, Edith now found herself struck by the crudeness of The Mount's gardens and the 'dishevelled' look of the New England landscape in 1903. The following summer, in England, she was so overwhelmed by the combination of natural and man-made beauty at Cambridge that she wondered if it might actually be demoralising for Americans to see it and realise what they lacked.

By 1906, her comparisons and criticisms of America had become almost ludicrous and the tone she took suggested they were a proxy for quite different dissatisfaction. Her marriage with Teddy had never brought real intimacy or happiness and was now becoming increasingly difficult. She identified America with Teddy, with all its unhappiness and constraints, and idealised Europe as her escape – fulfilling and beautiful.

Early on, while working for the Whartons on The Mount, Edith's friend Ogden Codman watched as Teddy suffered an attack of the mental illness that would eventually conquer him. Codman remembered too that Teddy's father had committed suicide in a mental hospital. On this occasion, Teddy was himself admitted to a mental hospital, but emerged, apparently recovered. However, although the couple continued, apparently happily, travelling and living together in Lenox and Paris, entertaining guests, running their estate and, in Edith's case, writing, beneath the surface all was not well. Wharton later admitted that she had felt a constant nausea, like seasickness, and a terrible tiredness throughout the twelve years of her marriage; Teddy's condition was worsening and, despite trying a number of recommended cures, Edith became increasingly aware that her husband was mentally ill.

In *The Reckoning* (1902), Wharton describes the living death of a marriage:

> Her husband's personality seemed to be closing gradually in on her, obscuring the sky and cutting off the air, till she felt herself shut up among the decaying bodies of her starved hopes.[14]

She was haunted, no doubt, by her fears that this disloyalty might be the cause of Teddy's ill health and that her success as a writer, and her circle of eminent friends, with whom he had little in common, had brought about her husband's sad state. She was trapped in a vicious circle of assertion, guilt and self-doubt, which raged within her as she and Teddy visited specialists throughout Europe and America and tried to find a cure for his illness.

Early in 1907, Wharton's life took an unexpected and dramatic turn when she fell in love with Morton Fullerton, an exciting, bisexual, American journalist with a highly chequered past. Fullerton lived in Paris and worked for *The Times* and *The Times Literary Supplement*; he was well connected and well read. He fitted in with Wharton's friends as a good friend of Robert Norton and a fellow student at Harvard with Wharton's friend, the art historian Bernard Berenson. Above all, he was a friend of her great friend Henry James (although he came with something of a warning from that source). Wharton and Fullerton met socially in Paris and got on well – they shared a professional involvement in publishing and both were well travelled and well read – and Fullerton could have joined the ranks of her other close male friends, were it not for an incident in New England. Henry James came to stay with the Whartons at Lenox and Edith invited Fullerton to join them; but he came instead in October, when Henry James had gone. Indeed, his ostensible reason for coming was that he was giving a lecture on Henry James at nearby Bryn Mawr College and would stay at The Mount overnight. The Whartons had other guests staying and Edith made up a small party, including Fullerton, to drive in the Berkshire Hills (typically, Teddy was unwell and did not join them). It had snowed in the night and, as their road rose over the hills, the chauffeur had to stop to put on chains. As they waited by the roadside, Wharton and Fullerton smoked and talked and noticed a small bush of witch hazel in flower in the snow.

The small incident affected Wharton deeply and she wrote to Sally Norton telling her, naively, what a wonderful drive they had had:

> A dazzling sun across blue mountains, through arches and
> long vistas of gold & amber...
>
> November 1907

She was in love.

When Fullerton's thank-you letter arrived, it enclosed a sprig of witch hazel. Wharton began a journal called *L'Âme Close* ('The Secret Soul'). The journal, she said, was her imaginary way of writing to Fullerton, but it was of course an outlet for her explosion of emotion. Exhilarated, transformed and madly in love, she persuaded Teddy to lock up Lenox early and they returned to Paris, where Fullerton awaited them. There was formal socialising: visits to the theatre and to lectures, all without Teddy, who was suffering with ill health. When he left Paris for a rest in Cannes, Wharton experienced with Fullerton a domestic happiness and contentment of which she had only dreamed. The couple met furtively and frequently in a series of outings, which she chronicled in her journal. The tone is almost embarrassingly adolescent in its observation of herself and her passions. As she was experiencing her first sexual pleasures, she felt all the wonder of discovery, which she put into words to store them for a future novel. At the same time, she was poignantly aware that the feelings would not last, and nor would the affair.

The experience had a huge influence on her writing, and her two powerful novellas *Ethan Frome* (1911) and *Summer* (1917) would not have been written without the knowledge and experience of what it was to feel love breathing life into a soul. But, as in the fiction, life was to take a painful turn. Fullerton was an unfaithful lover and was having an affair with his adopted sister at the same time as he was courting Wharton. As his ardour began to wane, so her letters went unanswered. Wharton's grief was so intense that in a letter to Henry James she describes herself as virtually suicidal. To Fullerton she wrote that, having been introduced to happiness, she could not now return to her former imprisonment. When she arrived in New York and met Teddy, she felt 'The key turn in my prison lock...'[15]

Gradually, she found the strength and means to live again and poured her misery into her writing. Yet her situation was unsustainable and much as she wanted to avoid divorce as she struggled with misgivings over the morality of it, she had to consider the possibility. She had successfully satirised the subject in her novel from this period, *The Custom of the Country* (1913), in which the provincial Undine Spragg makes her way up the social ladders of New York and Europe through a series of divorces; but while this is dealt with satirically, the pain and destructive damage of divorce is acknowledged in the suicide of

Spragg's husband, Ralph Marvell. Although Wharton felt she had the right to end the disastrous and unhappy marriage to Teddy, she had been brought up to regard divorce as socially unacceptable and a divorcee, like her heroine Ellen Olenska in *The Age of Innocence*, to be a social outcast. While she rejected this value system, and although the times themselves were changing in the public's attitude to divorce and divorcees, Wharton still saw divorce as problematic. In *The Custom of the Country* it leads to suicide and in *The Reckoning* the wife is discarded when she grows older, by which time she has lost herself to a passionate dependence on her husband.

Unable to find a way out of their predicament and the misery of her marriage, Wharton suggested they should sell The Mount, the scene of so much hope and the reality of so much disappointment; but she and Teddy could not agree. He wanted to hang on to it, and the house became a symbol of the miserable chains tying her to her husband, until their impasse was broken by a bizarre confession from Teddy that he had embezzled $50,000 of his wife's money to spend on his mistress.

They were divorced the following year in Paris; divorcing in France spared the Whartons some of the publicity there would have been in the States. Meanwhile, though her affair with Fullerton continued, it lacked much of the earlier intensity and, by 1914, Wharton felt very much her own woman again. Planning to take an English country house for a summer of friends and exploration, her plans were thrown by the outbreak of war.

* * *

The First World War, which Wharton saw out in Paris rather than escaping to America, was in many ways a wonderful opportunity for her, though she had little time for writing. She sensed some of this herself in a letter to Bernard Berenson in August 1914: 'It is all thrillingly interesting but very sad…'

Living in Paris and witnessing the floods of fleeing Belgian refugees coming into the city, Wharton threw herself into voluntary work, using her wealthy contacts in France and the States to buy properties to house and feed them and raising money herself by writing an account of life in wartime Paris for *Scribner's Magazine*. In addition to seeing to the basic needs of the refugees, she established training facilities, clinics, clothing exchanges, nurseries and reading rooms, sewing rooms and sanatoria for thousands of French and Belgians. Unlike many rich Parisians she remained in Paris, even when it shut down for fear of the German invasion, and, like Cocteau and Maugham, she visited the Front as a voluntary medical worker, bringing supplies to cut-off hospitals where the conditions were horrendous.

In a letter to Henry James, she describes a visit to Verdun with her chauffeur, Cook:

> Picture this all under a white winter sky, driving great flurries of snow across the mud-&-cinder-coloured landscape, with the steel cold Meuse winding between beaten poplars – Cook standing with Her *[her car]* in a knot of mud-coated military motors & artillery horses, soldiers coming & going, cavalrymen riding up with messages, poor bandaged

creatures in rag-bag clothes leaning in doorways, & always, over and above us, the boom, boom, boom of the guns on the grey heights to the east. It was Winter war to the fullest, just in that little insignificant corner of the immense affair.

14 May 1915

Her accounts from the Front were published by *Scribner's* and helped Wharton raise funds for her charities, but also raised awareness among Americans of the situation in Europe, a war in which they were not yet playing a part.

They were also collected into a book called *Fighting France, from Dunkerque to Belfort* (1915), which was well reviewed. Working as a relief worker and a war correspondent as well as running her charities was immensely tiring and gave her no time for her fiction. Yet to sustain her charities she had to keep writing her articles, and to cope with new emergencies she needed to find new means. She now set up another fund-raising venture, *The Book of the Homeless* (1916): a collection of poetry, prose, music, drawings and paintings by famous contributors whom Wharton persuaded to become involved. Thomas Hardy, John Galsworthy, Henry James, Joseph Conrad, Claude Monet, Auguste Renoir, John Singer Sargent, Jean Cocteau, Rupert Brooke and Auguste Rodin contributed original pieces of work. Rudyard Kipling and William Butler Yeats declined, for whatever reasons, though Kipling made a generous donation. Sales of the book, combined with special editions and the auction of the artwork, successfully raised funds of $9,500 (approximately $225,000 today) for Wharton's projects. By 1916 Wharton's reputation as a benefactor and heroine was recognised by the award of the Légion d'Honneur, an exceptional honour both for a woman and in wartime, but she was no longer in Paris to receive it. Exhausted by her war efforts, she had escaped to Hyères.

Summer is the novella that came out of this period back in the South of France: her emotional escape was the world of New England during the early part of her marriage. It is the New England not of Wharton's smart set but of the 'left behind', living, or slowly dying, like Ethan Frome, in forgotten and isolated villages, amid a scenery that is beautiful in summer but murderous in winter. The characters are materially poor and emotionally starved. Incest as well as poverty are two of the themes of the novel. It is also an important female 'coming of age' story about Charity Royall, who displays a poignant mixture of knowingness and ignorance: hers is another form of the innocence with which Wharton plays in her next long novel. The imagery of the novel is natural and fertile, and when Charity and Lucius walk together the countryside is transformed:

> The rounding of pale green cones on countless spruce-branches, the push of myriads of sweet-fern fronds in the cracks of the stony slope ... and the crowding shoots of meadow sweet and yellow flags ... All this bubbling of sap and slipping of sheaths and bursting of calyxes was carried to her on mingled currents of fragrance.[16]

And yet the novella owed more to the war than perhaps Wharton herself realised. Visiting the Front, she described, in *Fighting France*, the bombs exploding like tropical flowers. In *Summer*, Lucius pulls Charity into their first embrace at a firework display where the 'whole night broke into flower'.

The predominant mood is happiness and even the potential tragedy of the ending is transformed to a degree by realism and pragmatism into some sort of gentle and ironic triumph. It is apt that it should have been inspired in part by the destruction of the war and the miraculous rebirth of coming to Hyères. When the war finally ended and Wharton was able to think about taking up her own life again, she turned to the peace and inspiration she had found in Hyères. She stayed there to look for a house in January 1919 and described her life to Bernard Berenson:

> I read your letter 'stretched on a bank of amaranth & moly', with the blue sea sending little silver splashes up to my toes, & roses & narcissus & mimosa outdoing Coty's best from the centre all round to the sea. In front of us lay two or three Odyssean isles, & the boat with a Lotean sail which is always in the right place was on duty as usual – & this is the way all my days are spent! Seven hours of blue-&-gold & thyme & rosemary & hyacinth & roses every day that the Lord makes: & in the evenings, dozing over a good book.
>
> 27 January 1919

Wharton, who had swung for years between her two identities and nationalities – American and French – had, at last, decided that she belonged in France. Perhaps the war had persuaded her that this was her home, and she now set about settling properly and acquiring not one but two houses. The first, outside Paris, had already been bought when she came to Hyères to search for a winter home and rented, on a long lease, Sainte-Claire, a former convent built into the ruins of the old castle. It stood atop a hill, with long sloping gardens, which she saw transformed immediately in her imagination. Meanwhile, she was content to enjoy the garden, the roses and narcissus and mimosa. The warmth, the golden colour of the scenery and the windless calm of the surroundings seemed to her almost miraculous in the wake of the horrors of war. At last able to come to terms with herself and the failure of her marriage, she felt ready to start again and so set about creating a home with roots for this new chapter of her life. Here, she could write and entertain her friends; and, by settling in France, she could live away from the social constraints and disapproval of American society.

Although a wealthy woman, her house outside Paris and her house in Hyères were costly projects to run. Wharton therefore sat down to earn herself the means to indulge her hobbies and began to write her greatest novel, *The Age of Innocence*. Like Katherine Mansfield, Wharton reacted to the devastations of the war by a return to her youth and set the novel in 1870s New York, a world that had disappeared just as surely as pre-war Europe. In a letter to her publisher and friend Charles Scribner, Wharton described how impossible it was now to write a novel set immediately before the outbreak of war:

I seem to have forgotten how people felt and what their point of view was.

12 September 1919

Unlike Mansfield, who felt that the trauma of the war meant it was no longer possible to write in a traditional style, Wharton did not feel the need to create a new form for her narrative, and she completed her novel within a year. Once again, the plot centred on tension between European and American cultures and behaviour; once again her main characters were imprisoned by the tight conformity of their class and clan, and once again every action taken and *not* taken was noted by the watchful eyes of society. The novel dealt with the familiar subject of divorce, but not American social ambition as in *The Custom of the Country*; rather, it hinted at European domestic abuse. The irony of the novel lies in all that is understood and not said – as in the novels of her late friend Henry James. However, where James is dark and sinister, *The Age of Innocence* purposefully steers away from the melodrama of Wharton's earlier novels. The novel creates an ironic and complex balance of tensions in which the values of old New York are not destroyed or undermined even as they are exposed and questioned. By the time she came to write it, Wharton's anger at New York society seems to have abated and the novel's tone, if not its subject matter, is quietly redemptive and accepting.

Wharton couldn't have asked for a better reception to the novel: it became an immediate bestseller and was acclaimed in literary circles. Wharton was awarded the Pulitzer Prize, the first woman to be so honoured, and an honorary degree at the all-male Yale University. The income enabled her to begin work on the house at Hyères, and when she finally moved in for her first Christmas in 1920, it was the simple pleasure of the house and its views that brought her immense happiness.

Establishing a garden at Hyères was an enormous under-taking: she supervised the building of a series of gardens on the rocky slopes in between writing her novels and articles. As usual, she gave much thought to the critical relation between the house, the garden and the surrounding landscape – in this case the *maquis*, the scrubby, rocky land just inland from the Mediterranean, which is a natural home to thyme, rosemary and lavender but is far from fertile. She had first to improve the infrastructure of her site with drainage and irrigation; then she had to plan for shade and shelter, for the Hyères climate was often harsh in winter as well as dry in summer. She brought in topsoil; hired labourers and gardeners; built terraces and pergolas and ordered plants in their thousands to create her beloved drifts of opulence. Like many gardens in the South of France, it had its olives and cypress trees, its agaves and exotic succulents, and she experimented with unusual plants – new discoveries from China or Latin America. For most of her visitors, it was the colour of her flowers and shrubs that was overwhelming – blue hyacinths in winter, followed by orange freesias in spring and, in summer, roses climbing over walls and arches, pergolas and outbuildings. The garden was written up in *Country Life* as one of the very best of the Riviera. Yet her friend Daisy Chanler, struggling to describe its beauty, probably gets closer to the heart of the creation than *Country Life*, seeing the garden as very much the reflection of its owner:

> Her garden is somehow an image of her spirit, of her inmost self. It shows her love of beauty, her imagination, her varied knowledge and masterly attention to detail; like her it was somehow inaccessible. Her garden is a symbol of the real Edith.[17]

Writing a preface to Alice Martineau's *Gardening in Sunny Lands*, Wharton describes the excitement a gardener from the north feels on acquiring a Mediterranean garden where they can grow plants that need a greenhouse or much mollycoddling at home. In an unpublished essay entitled 'A French Riviera Garden in the Spring', she describes:

> When the peaches and cherries are in bloom, and all the late tulips, narcissi, ranunculus, anemones and irises come rushing up mingling with roses, lilacs and paeonies to swell the mighty chorus.

Entertaining at Sainte-Claire involved sitting on wicker chairs on the generous terrace. The house had seven bedrooms and six bathrooms, and the style was less formal than in her previous home in a Paris apartment. There were four reception rooms opening onto the terrace and a library, cool and shaded from the sun, in which her collections were carefully arranged. Just as she had done at The Mount, Wharton invited only people she wanted to see and provided a comfortable and generous holiday for them. As she had done at The Mount, she kept her guests to her strict schedule: she worked in bed until 11 a.m. and there would then be a good lunch on the terrace, or perhaps a picnic in the country, with drives to local beauty spots like Grasse or further afield to Uzès, Pont du Gard, Avignon. She loved showing her friends the beauties of the area and of her garden; but she also loved the evenings, with long conversations on books and people as well as readings from Trollope, Jane Austen and George Eliot, and occasionally from Wharton's work in progress, such as *The Old Maid* (1924). These sessions, she claimed, were very helpful, though whether she took any notice of the advice of those she called her 'Patient Listeners' is doubtful. Guests remarked on her relaxed state, her great fits of laughter, often at 'unsuitable' topics, and how different she was from the rather distant dowager of her public persona. She was shy and this often showed itself in a superiority and distance with strangers that her real friends did not recognise.

There were famously awful evenings, too, such as with Scott Fitzgerald, a neighbour in the South of France as well as a rival in the world of American bestsellers, or Cocteau, to whom she revealed her contempt for modern art. With Huxley, whose family she knew well, she was friendly though distant, but she had not lost her gift for making friends with younger people. Philomène de Lévis-Mirepoix, who was twenty-five years her junior, became a close friend, as did Kenneth Clark, the young curator of the National Gallery in London. He and his wife, Jane, were frequent guests and Wharton became godmother to their son Colin. Her neighbour and fellow garden expert, the Comte de Noailles, became a friend with whom she could discuss plants and garden design, although his style was aggressively modern. She went on garden visits to the great gems of the Riviera, to Hanbury across the border in Italy and Serre de la Madone in Menton, as well as to her friend Ogden Codman's palace, La Leopolda, and other great gardens on Cap Ferrat.

Her years in Hyères would prove to be some of her happiest. She wrote some of her most experimental novels – *The Children* (1928), *The Old Maid* and *New Year's Day* (1924) – all deeply unsettling and tackling unpopular subjects such as illegitimacy and prostitution, previously only hinted at in *The Age of Innocence*. Like Newland Archer's wife, May, Delia Ralston is an outwardly obedient wife; but where there is ambiguity as to how much May knew of her husband's love for Ellen (her cousin), and how instrumental she was in foiling their relationship, in *The Old Maid* Wharton takes us into Delia's thoughts and decisions and allows us to follow her apparently benign but essentially destructive relationship with her cousin, Charlotte, and Charlotte's illegitimate daughter. Although the setting of the novella is again 1870s New York society, with its codes and taboos, the content of the short story is essentially modern and deals with Delia's growing awareness of the complexities of her own personality and the degree to which she has sacrificed these to more comfortable social expectations. Her cousin, Charlotte, meanwhile, single, poor and pitiful, has experienced the overwhelming passion of sexuality and has managed to stay true to her own values and beliefs despite an enormous sacrifice. We are shown the deadly duality of generosity and the delusions of morality with a violence that makes the reading shocking and yet totally gripping and overwhelmingly twentieth century.

In *New Year's Day*, Wharton describes Mrs Hazeldean, a former prostitute who lived by her own moral code, in her older age:

> Mrs Hazeldean's society consisted mainly of men, men of all ages, from her bald or grey-headed contemporaries to youths of Hubert's accomplished years and raw novices of mine.
>
> A great dignity and decency prevailed in her little circle. It was not the reformed respectability which weighs on the reformed declassee, but the air of ease imparted by a woman of distinction who has wearied of society and closed her doors to all save her intimates.[18]

When she was a very young girl, and before she had learned to read, Wharton would 'make up'. This compulsive pastime involved her holding an open book and telling a story she had made up as she walked around the house. So obsessive was this activity that she refused to stop even when invited friends came for tea, and would ask her mother to entertain them on her behalf. In this behaviour we can see the adult Wharton and her deep-seated need to write stories, together with her impatience with conventional expectations of friendship and her desire to find her own friends. Independent both socially and financially, Wharton achieved much of the peace and calm she enjoyed in her later years in Hyères through her own determination. Doubtless there were many sacrifices, but she triumphed in her friendships and her works.

WILLIAM SOMERSET
MAUGHAM

———◆———

He finished reading his post and folded his day-old copy of *The Times.* The news was good: the latest revival of his play had opened to tremendous reviews in the West End and Noel had sweetly sent him a note of congratulations. He was coming down to Cannes for a few days and hoped Maugham and his secretary, Haxton, would be able to motor over to join him. Meanwhile, from New York his agent sent the list of theatrical impresarios and producers he had lined up to meet him when he came over for the opening of his new Broadway show. From California came news that Hollywood producers were fighting over the movie rights to his short stories and queuing to meet him when he came out West. Humming somewhat tunelessly, Maugham checked his appearance in the full-length mirror by the door of his study and, flicking an imaginary speck from his immaculate white duck trousers and smoothing back his hair, he made his careful way down the green stairs that led into the main part of the house. Just off the black-slated entrance hall, his 'companion' and secretary, Gerald Haxton, was typing up the morning's work.

'What do you think of it so far? Not bad?'

Gerald, pausing to turn in his chair, nodded his approval.

'I rather like it. It's quite unusual and the characters are really beginning to come alive. Another masterpiece, *Master*!'

'Let's hope so, Gerald, let's hope so. Meanwhile, you Americans are biting, it seems, and we will have a round of meetings in New York next month.'

In the book-filled drawing room, the afternoon sun streamed through open French windows. It was October, but still warm enough for drinks in the courtyard before dinner and sufficiently cool for a fire to be laid ready in the enormous stone fireplace decorated with a huge gilded eagle. He was entertaining three Russian princesses for dinner that night – an occasion for them to show off their gleaming fur shawls and wraps before dinner and their sparkling emeralds and diamonds at the table. He had arranged the menu days before with Annette, his cook: something light and feminine, but not too bland for the taste buds.

Maugham walked out onto his terrace; it was framed by tightly clipped hedges and dotted with shade-giving palms, swaying gently in the sea breeze. America seemed a long way away from the hillside of Cap Ferrat, looking down towards the sea – slashes of dark blue between the trunks of the pine trees. Wood pigeons called from the thick foliage, mingling their calls with the rhythmic sounds of a rake smoothing the gravel ready for his guests. It was close to perfection and a long way from the rectory where he lived with his penny-pinching aunt and uncle, with their petty provincial ways, after the death of his parents. Perhaps it was those bleak rectory dinners – his uncle at the head of the meagre table, his aunt expectant in her black silk best gown, and he, Willie, stammering nervously under the pressure of a question – that led to his love of entertaining now.

The Villa La Mauresque was perfect for entertaining; his house parties were reported in society columns and even the out-of-season dinners, like tonight's, had acquired, he was pleased to say, a note of glamour. He enjoyed the company of titled ladies, even if they had fallen on hard times, and the civilised bonhomie of the people one met, here in the South of France, had much to commend it. One of the great virtues of the Côte d'Azur was that people knew how to behave, were ready to 'sing for their supper' and sparkle at the small talk, not like some of those insufferably tedious young men who came out from England to meet the 'great writer' and had absolutely no idea how to make conversation over a luncheon table. They never got an invitation again.

'Strange', reflected Maugham, 'how even successful friends like Godfrey Winn had had to be shown the ropes, in what was expected of them while staying on the Riviera.'[19]

Winn had shown up on his first visit in a pair of grey flannels, as though this were Wimbledon or some such place, and he, Maugham, had had to have Gerald take him into Nice and kit him out in white duck trousers and espadrilles, *de rigueur* on the Côte d'Azur if you wanted to blend in. Gerald –

who, of course, never wanted to merge into the crowd – wore bright swimming shorts and striped matelot tops, but then Gerald was another matter.

It was time to go upstairs to change. Maugham glanced appreciatively at the Chinese statue of Kuan Yin, Goddess of Mercy, at the foot of the stairs and took the marble treads slowly so that he could admire his Siamese bronzes, brought back from his travels in the East. At the top of the stairs he turned towards his own room; his hand-painted Sicilian bed beckoned, but he resisted the urge to lie down and picked up the book he was reading instead. Below him, out of the corner windows, he could see his dogs being walked, Brunhilde straining at her leash and Parsifal holding back to follow up an alluring scent he had found. He hoped his guests liked dogs.

Later that evening, after the princesses had enjoyed their drinks in the courtyard, he would take them into the house and watch them look at things. How many people failed to appreciate or even notice the statues in the hall or the bronzes rising from the marble staircase. Nearly everyone could recognise some of the Impressionist paintings, but how many of them understood they were looking at a collection that was unique, not only in the individual pictures but in the accumulated wealth they represented. Then there were his Zoffanys and his famous Toulouse-Lautrec, which no one ever identified. *Le Raboteur* was a male nude and Maugham loved him all the more for the dealer's comment that it would have cost him three times as much if it had been a female. For that was Maugham's private joke – private at least when, as tonight, he was entertaining respectably, playing the charming host to titled ladies and a couple of wealthy neighbours. At other times, especially at his famous summer house parties, there was hardly a woman on the glittering guest list; instead, the tantalising half-promise of some rough trade, acquired by Gerald among the bars of Villefranche, a mere stone's throw – and a whole lifestyle away – from the grandeur and ceremony of Cap Ferrat.

Unkind commentators noted that four types of guest were welcome at Villa La Mauresque: the titled, the wealthy, the famous and the young and good-looking (men). Sometimes a guest managed to combine two or more of these characteristics, like the young Sir Francis Rose, who was the ward of Maugham's older brother (now the Lord Chancellor in Britain) and was staying with his mother, the medium Lady Rose, at the Hôtel Welcome in Villefranche, where Cocteau was giving him drawing lessons.

* * *

When Maugham came to live in the South of France, he was already hugely successful on both sides of the Atlantic as a best-selling novelist and an immensely popular playwright in the West End and on Broadway (he even achieved the distinction of having three plays running simultaneously). Not only was he the highest paid writer of his day but he was actually the highest paid ever, until Hollywood royalties distorted writers' incomes.

He was in his fifties and came to France to retire, reflect on his life, escape the pressures of the London social scene –

including his wife and daughter – and to write, mainly short stories, in the comparative calm of his secluded villa. Ten years on, in 1938, he published a sort of autobiography – *The Summing Up* – in which he looked back on his life as a writer and society figure in the pre-First World War years.

> *[it was a]* … Luxurious existence … the social round, the grand dinners at the houses of the great, the brilliant balls and the week-end parties at country houses; the company of clever and brilliant people, writers, painters, actors; the love affairs I had had and the easy companionship of my friends; the comfortableness and security of life.[20]

By the time he came to France that world had, of course, disappeared; but in some ways, moving to France allowed Maugham to recreate and perpetuate just that illusion of eternal Edwardian comfort, which depended on his considerable earned wealth and on the ready supply of relatively inexpensive servants (he had thirteen) to be found on the Riviera. His estate of 20 acres on Cap Ferrat – then, as now, one of the most beautiful parts of the Riviera, a secluded, wooded promontory jutting out into Villefranche Bay, between Nice and Monte Carlo – comprised pine woods, citrus groves, a tennis court and marble swimming pool, and the grand, remodelled villa in which he hung his impressive collection of paintings and oriental decorative art. Maugham's lavish house parties at La Mauresque were legendary and generous. In their cool bedrooms his guests found

77

baskets of fruit, bottles of water and headed writing paper; in the bathrooms were expensive colognes and soaps from Floris.

While they stayed at the villa, his friends enjoyed a secluded and self-contained world with Maugham as its lord and centre, surrounded by a glittering cross section of British society: the writer and actor Noël Coward, the writers and journalists Godfrey Winn and Beverley Nichols, the art historian and millionaire Kenneth Clark, the magnate Lord Beaverbrook and his house guest Winston Churchill were all visitors, and so too were Harold Nicolson, Cecil Beaton, Cyril Connolly, Evelyn Waugh, Artur Rubinstein, Bob Boothby, Ian Fleming, Chips Channon, Moira Shearer, Sibyl Colefax, John Gielgud, George Cukor and Raymond Mortimer. Maugham entertained actors and playwrights, photographers and artists, politicians and journalists – serious thinkers and popular writers, good-looking men and an occasional beautiful actress were all accustomed to meet at Maugham's pampering house parties.

Arriving on Cap Ferrat by road, guests would spot, painted on the gateposts of the villa, Maugham's motif for good luck, which also decorated his books and had become his personal logo. It was, as he often told people, an image from his childhood, an amulet brought back from North African travels by his father and treasured for both its personal and cultural associations. On Cap Ferrat it marked Maugham's territory, like the flag of a kingdom. Sweeping up the drive to the villa, visitors would gaze in wonder at lush green lawns, banks of blue flowering agapanthus and tightly clipped hedges. The whole scene was calculated to impress – this was no ordinary author but a great man of letters, surrounded by his priceless possessions and served by a retinue of servants in a style befitting royalty. The villa, when his guests reached it, was also perfection: simple, low-lying and green-shuttered, it hinted at promises rather than overwhelming with its own presence. Built round a central courtyard in an Arabic style, the house looked outwards over the pines and palms of Maugham's garden down to the Mediterranean sea. The groves of oranges and lemons perfumed the air, mimosa and oleander flowered, there were shady walks and cooling fish ponds, and, for entertainment, the tennis court and the swimming pool decorated with classical marble statues.

In this Mediterranean kingdom, guests were greeted by footmen bearing trays of cold drinks as they lay by the pool or read under a palm tree. Loungers and ashtrays, parasols and fans appeared and were removed like props in one of Maugham's own plays.

Society columnists vied with each other to report stories from the poolside or the dining table or to catch glimpses of the celebrities arriving or leaving La Mauresque. Many of his guests, themselves writers, described their stay in letters home, as Harold Nicolson did in a letter to his wife, Vita:

> I am glad I came here. It really is the perfect holiday. I mean, the heat is intense, the garden lovely, the chair long and cool, the lime juice at hand, a bathing-pool there if one wishes to splash, scenery, books, gramophones, pretty people – and above all the sense that it is not going on too long.
>
> 14 August 1938

However, there's no such thing as a free lunch, and for this perfection there was a price: guests were expected to shine. Conversation around the courtyard lunch table or at the more formal dinner table had to sparkle. Maugham worked hard and expected his friends to do so too. Godfrey Winn, struggling to find his place as a writer, was soundly ticked off for taking the mornings off writing to enjoy himself in the sun. He had been generously invited for a month in the summer but not, as Willie pointed out to him, just because he was good at tennis and bridge but in order to have the time and space in which to write. His host wrote every morning, secluded in his writing room, from which he would emerge at midday for ice-cold cocktails on the terrace. Lunch would be taken in the courtyard and would often be rounded off with Maugham's celebrated avocado ice cream, made from fruit from his own trees, the only avocado trees on the Mediterranean! After lunch, Maugham might have a short siesta and then deal with his post and read the newspapers. In the afternoons his friends were allowed to relax and enjoy the garden and swimming pool. There were games of tennis and golf (Maugham enjoyed both) and trips on Haxton's yacht. As the first breath of the evening breeze set the palm fronds moving, the guests would reluctantly rouse themselves from their loungers and books and, with perhaps a glance at the sun setting dramatically in a pink sky, would go upstairs to bathe in Floris oils and to dress for dinner. Other guests – local duchesses or international tycoons – might come over for dinner and even the Duke and Duchess of Windsor eagerly accepted an invitation. Unless there was bridge, Maugham retired early to bed, where he read himself to sleep with a thriller. For the guests the night might still be young and, depending on the crowd, there could be trips to the casino at Monte Carlo or the seedy bars and gay nightlife of Villefranche.

Although the absence of women at his parties and the predominantly male atmosphere in which he lived and worked was, at the time, far more common than it is today and not necessarily an overt sign of sexual preference, there is no doubt that Maugham was bisexual and probably much more homosexual than he admitted to himself. As he confided to his nephew, Robin, towards the end of his life, his crucial mistake had been to think he was one-quarter 'queer' and three-quarters 'normal', whereas, he now realised, the reverse was true. Throughout his life he maintained a façade of carefully cultivated 'normality' and refused to add his name to the growing petitions for liberalisation of the anti-homosexual laws.

Twenty-one years old at the time of Oscar Wilde's trial and imprisonment, his sexuality was a source of constant personal fear of discovery; the trial was a turning point in British social history that exposed the hypocrisy and philistinism at the heart of the Establishment. Those homosexuals who could left England for more sympathetic countries, while those who remained lived in constant fear of exposure through entrapment or betrayal. The effect on a young man like Maugham, beginning to explore his own sexuality, must have been profound and disturbing. Denial was one way he developed to cope with his secret and shameful sexuality, and this involved a compensatory overemphasis of his heterosexual side. Judging by his writings, Maugham had a number of genuine, serious, sexual relationships with women early in his career as a writer. He was also a successful member of the fast-moving, promiscuous social whirl of fashionable London before the First World War. However, given the much more segregated society of the day, he had, in parallel, enjoyed frequent retreats into all-male company, whether in his gentlemen's clubs, on holidays on Capri or on the Front in northern France, where he went as an ambulance driver shortly after the outbreak of war (as did Cocteau, in a designer uniform).

It was probably also this aspect of pre-1914 life that Maugham tried to recreate at La Mauresque, where he could entertain all-male company, confident that his own quite old-fashioned conventions on behaviour would prevail. The behaviour of his partner, Gerald Haxton, in the bars of Villefranche was allegedly much less discreet. Haxton was an easy-going young American, an extrovert, whom Maugham had met originally when he, like Cocteau and Edith Wharton, had served in the ambulance corps. His opposite in many ways, Haxton complemented Maugham superbly. Where Maugham was reserved, Haxton was outgoing; where Maugham was ashamed and secretive about his sexuality, Haxton was comfortable and open about his. He probably introduced Maugham to a fulfilled sex life on their first long journey together in the South Pacific. The effect of that voyage on Maugham can be felt in the clarity and joyfulness of his prose in the collection of short stories he published afterwards. He said that he had gone to the South Seas:

Katherine Mansfield.
Portrait of the New Zealand author,
real name Kathleen Beauchamp.

Katherine Mansfield
standing in the garden
at the Villa Isola Bella,
Menton, France

Portrait of Jean
Cocteau in his studio
at Villa Santo Sospir
Saint-Jean-Cap-Ferrat,
Alpes-Maritimes

Jean Cocteau painting

Portrait of Jean Cocteau

Edith Wharton at
home on the Riviera

Edith Wharton at her writing desk

William Somerset
Maugham. Photographed
at his Villa La Mauresque,
Cap Ferrat, France, *c*.1948.

Winston Churchill,
Somerset Maugham and
H.G. Wells at Villa La
Mauresque, Maugham's
home on Cap Ferrat,
Côte d'Azur, Riviera.
France, April 1937.

F. Scott Fitzgerald with his wife, Zelda, and daughter, Scottie,
on the road, in France

F. Scott Fitzgerald with Zelda and Scottie on the French Riviera

Aldous Huxley, Matthew Huxley; Maria Huxley; Lady Ottoline Morrell

> ...looking for beauty and romance ... I found beauty and
> romance, but I also found something I had never expected.
> I found a new self...[21]

His writing conveys some of the excitement and clarity of his
discovery, the magical transformation of the world and its inhab-
itants under the influence of his love for Haxton. This rubbed
off onto the people he met — he found them larger, brighter and
more full of life than people at home.

> Now I entered a new world, and all the instinct in me of a
> novelist went out with exhilaration to absorb the novelty. It
> was not only the beauty of the islands that took me ... what
> excited me was to meet one person after another who was
> new to me. I was like a naturalist who comes into a country
> where the fauna are of an unimaginable variety...[22]

The characters he met in Malaysia, the South Seas and Indonesia
were immortalised in his writings and have become part of the
British colonial legacy. His *Writer's Notebook* for 1916 is bursting
with entries vividly describing the people he met and the lives
he imagined or heard them narrating. They are the archetypal
'expats', desperately homesick but unable to return due to
disgrace, lack of money or some other source of shame. Then
there are those who have come east in search of spiritual fulfilment but have become trapped in their no man's land between
worlds, accepted in neither and always yearning after the other.

The physical exile his characters suffer is mirrored, of course, in their psychological imprisonment and it is this that makes the stories so evocative and still so appealing today. There are the homesick exiles trapped in a sort of paradise – the punctilious government official secretly dreaming of West Kensington, the lonely Irish schoolmaster who came out for adventure and romance, and the French priest who talks about Shakespeare and Wordsworth. Others are escaping some shameful past, like the drunken hotelkeeper who was once a dentist in Newcastle or the insurance clerk who embezzled a fortune from his company. In the bars and hotels of the South Seas they mix with other flotsam, the expats who have 'gone native', such as Swan, the skipper, with his four native wives, or C., the Australian horse-trainer, with his half-caste baby.

Early in his career, when he was studying to be a doctor, Maugham had discovered himself as a writer by creating a novel based on the tragic but heroic lives of the slum dwellers of Lambeth he met through his work. Now, once again, he had found a rich new seam of human experience to mine for his fiction, and it is to his credit that he never appears to be judgemental, patronising or over-romantic.

This voyage in 1916 was the first of many Maugham and Haxton made together to exotic destinations that later feature as settings for Maugham's work. Together they visited Thailand, Tahiti, Tonga, Samoa, Fiji, Borneo, Korea, Burma, India, China, Malaysia, Singapore, Latin America and, nearer home, Spain and Italy. To Maugham, they were simply 'the best years of my life'.[23]

However, while Maugham and Haxton were finding love in the South Seas, Maugham's mistress, Syrie Wellcome, was in the midst of a very nasty divorce. Her husband, from whom she had long been separated, was taking the unusual step of suing his wife for divorce and naming Maugham as the co-respondent. In effect, this forced Maugham, as a man of honour, to marry Syrie to prevent her from being socially and financially destitute. Syrie was pregnant with Maugham's child and his duty was thus doubly clear. Nevertheless, he found it hard to accept his plight. Instead, to Syrie's dismay, he insisted he had to go to New York and then on a six-month trip with Haxton back to the South Seas to research his next novel, *The Moon and Sixpence* (1919), the life of Gaugin. If Syrie had found no one else to marry, he would marry her on his return. Syrie, who probably understood Maugham's sexuality better than he did, was prepared to put up with these harsh terms for the sake of her own and her daughter's reputations. She gambled, perhaps unwisely, that Maugham valued his reputation as a heterosexual too dearly to jeopardise it and with her he could safely guard his secret and pursue his passions as he wished.

In the event, they were married in New Jersey. For such a highly visible couple it was a small and hushed affair, planned doubtless to attract as little publicity as possible. Maugham's ambivalence over his marriage was clearly revealed: he would do the honourable thing, but he would do it with the least fuss and pleasure possible. To complicate matters, of course, there was Haxton, now his great love and furthermore, as a homosexual (with a past), banned from entering Britain. Perhaps Syrie had counted on that; perhaps Maugham, too, had imagined he could lead parallel lives, the family man in London with Syrie and the homosexual lover with Haxton abroad, on their oriental travels.

The Maughams kept up the pretence of their marriage for eleven years. They were helped at first by the war and Maugham's secret work for the government, which took him to Russia, and they were then separated by an attack of TB that kept him at a sanatorium in Scotland for some months, where he was a model patient and was eventually cured. This enforced separation during the first year of marriage was good for them, and when they were reunited they had an enjoyable and bucolic summer in 1917 *en famille* in a rented house outside Farnham, where Maugham rode and wrote *The Moon and Sixpence* and little Liza played happily in the garden. When he was well enough to leave the sanatorium permanently, they moved into Maugham's Mayfair house, where they had separate bedrooms but otherwise continued to live together. Haxton, who had come to England to visit his lover while he was ill, was deported as an undesirable.

The novel of that period, *The Moon and Sixpence*, handles a recurring theme – the tension between the artist's desire for self-fulfilment and his responsibilities to a wife and children. The strain between Maugham and Syrie was growing; they moved to a larger house in Marylebone to have more space and for Syrie to be near her shop in Baker Street, where she sold antiques and other furniture. As she became a successful interior designer with a good eye and an impressive client list, Maugham grew more and more critical and savaged her in public with his bitingly hurtful comments and sharp wit. Syrie was still desperate to find some way to keep the veneer of her marriage intact. She suggested they move to a house where Maugham could have his own front door and private apartments, so that they were living together in name only; she even went so far as to buy herself a house in northern France so that Haxton could join them for visits, but that venture ended disastrously. Maugham's decision to move to Cap Ferrat with Haxton was, in effect, his decision to leave Syrie. Within months of his move, Syrie asked him for a divorce.

France marked a significant turning point in Maugham's life, and it would provide the basis for his next novel, *Cakes and Ale* (1930). This is generally considered his greatest work and it is without doubt the sweetest and happiest in tone. Its story, suggested by Thomas Hardy's funeral, concerns a highly successful, eminent writer and distinguished 'man of letters' whose reputation rested on work he had completed in his youth under the influence of his first wife, Rosie, and their rackety lifestyle, which would, had it been known, have deeply shocked the respectable readership he had acquired and destroyed his reputation. The novel's central theme was the clash between a writer's private and public life. However, the strength of the novel and its impact on its readers lies in the character of Rosie, a promiscuous barmaid and one of the most complex and moving of all Maugham's characters.

Whatever the source of his inspiration – and many critics have identified Rosie as being based on Sue Jones, an early girl-friend of Maugham's – it is significant that he only managed to write about sexual gratification and promiscuity when he had moved away from England and found contentment with Gerald Haxton. Maugham remained, however, very much part of London society and the British literary scene and the immediate impact of *Cakes and Ale* was a massive game of 'hunt the clues' in the literary press as writers and critics vied to uncover the identities of the two writers in the novel, widely accepted to be Hardy and Hugh Walpole. The fallout of the novel in terms of hurt and unpleasantness was enormous. Walpole, though he claimed to be unaffected by it, was clearly wounded and so too was Hardy's widow and second wife, whose woman friend, Elinor Mordaunt, loyally wrote a scathing counter-attack on Maugham in her anonymous pastiche novel, *Gin and Bitters* (1931). She describes him as deeply unattractive physically...

> A small dark man, proud of his smallness; rather sallow, showing, even then, yellow pouches under his dark eyes: eyes as sad and disillusioned as those of a sick monkey.[24]

...and mentally he is portrayed as an ambitious snob, old and dissatisfied with life.

Maugham was sufficiently hurt by this attack to ask his brother, as a lawyer, to advise on a libel suit, but claimed not to have been in any way troubled by the novel, which failed to sell well in either Britain or America.

Yet times were changing. In the United States, 1929 brought the Wall Street Crash and although Maugham himself was unharmed by any losses in the stock market, many of his friends were ruined; the Riviera fell into decline and villas were left empty, while hotels and even casinos went out of business. In his next work – a play, *The Breadwinner* (1930) – Maugham had, as his main character, a bankrupt London stockbroker. The play was a comedy, the last he wrote, and in it he visited once again the theme of marriage. As in his novel *The Moon and Sixpence* (written under the influence of his early passion for Haxton), his protagonist leaves his wife and family to pursue self-fulfilment. However, in *The Breadwinner* there is considerable emphasis on the selfishness and greed of the wife and son, who are only interested in the stockbroker's money. While the dramatic treatment is funny, the play hides a deep undertone of hurt that may have reflected Maugham's feelings about Syrie (whose financial settlement he always resented) but is much more likely to reflect his preoccupation with a deterioration in his affair with Gerald Haxton.

Although Maugham had come to Cap Ferrat to be with Haxton, he was increasingly afraid that Haxton no longer recip-rocated his love and feared that the attraction was mercenary. In *A Writer's Notebook* he includes these 'Lines', written in 1929.

> *I could not bear the thought that I should ever lose you*
> *Or that our lives might ever be disjoined,*
> *But yet I know that in your wanton heart*
> *There was for me nor love nor tenderness.*
> *To many another I saw you give unwanted kisses,*
> *But when I sought to break the chain that bound me*

You twined your slim arms round my neck
And would not let me go.
Humbly I thanked you when you feigned to love me.
I bought your grudging lips for gold.
And now the love I thought would last till death is dead.
… I regret
My pain, my rapture, my anguish and my bliss.[25]

Maugham does not say to whom the 'Lines' were written and although the theme of unreciprocated love and the image of bondage are, of course, familiar from his early autobiographical novel *Of Human Bondage* (1915) (an exploration of an abusive heterosexual relationship), there is no reason to conclude that he is referring to that affair in this moving poem. Rather, the mention of bribery and buying of love suggests that the affair he is writing about happened when Maugham was wealthy, and in that case one must assume is about his relations with Haxton.

Haxton was an excessive drinker, which undoubtedly contributed to his relatively early death in 1944 at the age of fifty-two. His self-destructive behaviour (he was also a gambler) was perhaps born of the terrible tensions in his relationship with Maugham and his sense of inferiority in that relationship. At times the two men seemed, to observers, to be pitting all their energies into hurting each other. Haxton's personality was excessive, while Maugham's was moderate; he was a spendthrift while Maugham was careful with money, reckless where Maugham was cautious. They could complement each other delightfully or goad each other into ever worse displays of viciousness. At times, Maugham's friends were shocked at Haxton's abusive attitude to his partner and benefactor and his public humiliation of 'the Master'. Robin, Maugham's nephew, was one of the few friends who genuinely liked Haxton and appreciated how much he did for his uncle, and it was Maugham who realised how Haxton suffered in his role as companion and secretary to the 'great man' and forgave him his promiscuity and drunken binges as a safety valve. Yet Maugham felt that nothing had grown in the vacuum left by the loss of passion.

Spent is my passion
Like a river dried up by the sun's fierce rays.
I look into my empty heart and shrink dismayed:
My soul is like a desert and the wild wind blows
In its silent barren spaces.[26]

With the outbreak of war between Britain and Germany, Maugham was forced to leave France and greatly enjoyed the adventure of his escape on a collier bound for Britain. Haxton, meanwhile, as an American, was relatively safe and stayed behind at the villa, where he secreted the valuables and secured what remained. The couple were eventually reunited in America but by this time the United States was actively involved in the war and Haxton volunteered to join the war effort, while Maugham found accommodation through his American publisher. When Haxton became ill with pneumonia, Maugham rushed to his side and found him the best doctors and carers, but sadly to no avail, and Haxton died in 1944. Maugham eventually returned to Cap Ferrat and his house, so safely protected by Haxton. He had a new companion and lover, Alan Searle, but things were never quite the same again.

Many of his friends were dead or unable to travel; without Haxton, the light-hearted atmosphere of the early years could not be recaptured; and, above all, Maugham was growing old and cantankerous. His last years were unhappy and lonely, and he was constantly warring over money with Syrie and Liza.

His legacy was the dreamlike reality of those house parties, with all the wit and elegance of taste and culture, and his brilliantly evocative novels and short stories, which have never gone out of fashion.

F. SCOTT FITZGERALD

F. Scott Fitzgerald opened the door of his garden studio and stretched his body, stiff from sitting at his desk, into the warmth of the afternoon sun. In the garden of his French villa, bougainvillea bloomed in bright splashes against the stone walls and butterflies fluttered among the lavender bushes that bordered the steps leading down to the gate. His writing was going well. Behind him in the studio, the pages of the new chapter of *Gatsby* were neatly piled on the desk and they were good. He felt a rush of gratitude for the South of France, this blessed place, which had restored him as a writer and a person. In New York and New Jersey he had been a celebrity, but the peace he needed to write well had eluded him. Here, in Saint-Raphaël, this ordinary village of red-roofed houses with an air of suppressed carnival about them, tumbling gently towards the sea,[27] he had managed to find himself as a writer again, to create the story he had wanted to write for so long: the story of a man whose life was built on a dream.

The little house he and Zelda had rented in Valescure slept in the sun, the shutters closed to keep the rooms cool. He

picked up his swimming things and closed the doors, disturbing a gecko, which slid out of sight. Walking through the striped
shade of the pine forest, Scott pondered on how good the South
of France had been. It had been a risk, leaving America, but
it had paid off handsomely for them all and, oddly, the further he
was from home, the easier it seemed to write about it, as though
his imagination replaced the absent reality. There were very few
things about home that he missed, he realised – friends, perhaps,
more than anything else, and he knew that Zelda was probably
growing bored now the novelty of the first weeks playing at being
a French housewife had worn off. That was why he was so glad
she had managed to meet people on the beach – a crowd of
young French army officers, flyers, from Fréjus just up the road,
who reminded Zelda of all the aviators (like Scott) she had met
in Montgomery, Alabama, during the war. Some of the officers
were coming to dinner that evening, and they would eat outside
on the terrace in the welcome cool of the night to the reproach-
ful sound of the cicadas and, if they were lucky, the song of the
nightingale in the pine trees at the end of the garden.

As he turned the corner to come out at the bay he marvelled,
as he did every day, at the natural beauty of the spot; the mauve
hillsides of the protective bay cradled the brilliant blue sea,
fringed with exotic palm trees along the front. There was something quaint in the innocent charms of the place, an old-world
safety that you could still find, unexpectedly, in France, the
country that had lost so much of its innocence in the war. All
along the beach families were coming down to the sand now,

spreading out towels and opening picnics, the children running into the water while the parents took advantage of the respite from the working day to stretch out in the sun, or smoke a pipe. Scott spotted his own family, dark brown from their days on the beach, little Scottie like a native child running up from the sea towards Zelda, lying under a parasol. He ran to join them, scooping Scottie up in his arms and rushing with her down to the sea, pretending to throw her into the water, while she screamed in mock terror and delight. The sea had all the warmth and light of the Mediterranean day. Zelda was an excellent swimmer. She joined them now in the water and then struck out alone, straight towards the horizon, lost in the flat expanse of blue.

Later, watching her come out of the sea, Scott thought of the fiery southern belle he had married just after the war, when his bestselling debut novel, *This Side of Paradise* (1920), had shot him to the peak of New York society and had made them, for a while, the most sought-after couple in town. There had been parties and photographers, cocktails and nightclubs – all so new and so daring – and they had been the centre of it all, running hand in hand, stopping the traffic, down Fifth Avenue; dancing in the fountains outside The Plaza; turning cartwheels in the lobby of their honeymoon hotel. Everything had been new then – there was jazz to discover, a whole forbidden world of negro beats and seductive rhythms; there were the new women, 'flappers', he had christened them, with their bobbed hair, long legs under short skirts and flat chests like boys. Every day it seemed they discovered something new – a new drink, a new artist, a new party. He had summed up the era as 'the Jazz Age', a name that suggested the music, the heat, the sex that simmered just beneath the cocktails and the bars that were opening everywhere.

Just as some of the magic of those years began to grow stale, little Scottie had arrived and he and Zelda, children themselves, were suddenly parents – a whole generation older and quite lost as to how to do it, only knowing they did not want to be like their own parents. They had moved out of Manhattan to Long Island, where prosperous families lived and where they could raise little Scottie – or she could raise them, and turn them into grown-ups.

Coming to France had been about growing up. He and Zelda could never decide whose idea it was, but both had been willing.

'Life's so boring,' Zelda complained. 'Long Island can't be all there is, can it?'

She eyed her suitcases wistfully, longing to be on the move and away.

For Scott there was the recurrent dream of finding somewhere he could live cheaply, so cheaply he could give up the magazine articles that distracted him from his serious writing. There had been times, back home, when he was haunted by the fear that he might never be able to write anything worthwhile again. Those were the nights he went out and got properly drunk, coming home unconscious, his face bloody and his coat stained. Sometimes there were nights in police cells, and, when he came home, huge rows with Zelda, rows in which he threw things at her and she screamed and little Scottie watched them both, silent and afraid.

But on other days they were as happy as ever, daring each other to greater and funnier displays, making fun of the old-fashioned and the stuffy; amusing their friends. There were always the parties and sometimes it seemed that life was all parties, in galleries and cocktail bars, on boats and in ball-rooms; everyone they knew was having a party and lots of those whom they did not know wanted to meet them. Until they got so bored and so tired that Scott kept falling asleep at dinner tables and it was no longer amusing, just sad and bad, and it was time to move on.

* * *

The Americans they had met in France were unlike the crowd they ran with in New York. In Paris the expats were more serious – people like Gerald Murphy, an artist who knew all the painters and musicians. Gerald and his wife, Sara, had introduced Scott and Zelda to so many interesting people and they were coming down to the Riviera for the summer, doubtless bringing a crowd of really stimulating friends with them. Sara intrigued Scott – she was a new type of woman, quite unlike the flappers he had written so much about, with their girlish dizziness and artificial brightness. Sara seemed much more poised and sure of herself; she did not need to play at being fashionable, she was so perfect being herself – a mother, wife and hostess, but also an interesting person in her own right. Gerald and Sara were an ideal couple – highly educated, very rich Americans, who understood and participated in modern French culture.

The Murphys and their children came down to the South of France in August. They had taken over the whole floor of a hotel in Antibes, persuading the owner to keep the place open for them and their friends as an experiment to see if the summer season would work. They drove over to visit Scott and Zelda, where they met Edouard Josanne, Scott and Zelda's particular aviator friend, at supper, and went with them afterwards to the casino, where the band was playing that summer's song, 'Yes! We Have No Bananas'. It was everywhere that year. Afterwards, sitting on the terrace, Gerald said to Scott,

'How is Zelda? How is she filling her time while you are busy writing?'

Scott imagined, not Zelda but, conversely, Sara: Sara naked except for the long string of pearls she wore down her back when she was sunbathing, their opaque gleam setting off the colour of her skin.

In the silence, he realised Gerald was waiting for an answer, and something about his demeanour made Scott stiffen involuntarily, so that he was, when he came to it, almost ready for the blow. Almost, but not quite – never quite ready for it, for something like that.

'We are worried,' Gerald continued, unwrapping one of his legs and folding it over the other, 'worried that Zelda may be… how shall I put it?'

His delicacy seemed to protect him, but he was too honest to hide behind cliché, too good a friend to be silent.

'It looks to us, Scott, and heavens, you know her much better than we do – it seems as though she and that Frenchman, Josanne, are rather close.'

As though a blind had been pulled up and light now came streaming in through the window, Scott searched his friend's face for a sign of a joke. There was none. Gerald was still talking.

'You have been very preoccupied, understandably, of course, no doubt of that, but she has perhaps been neglected.'

Scott's instinct was to get up and smash his fist into his friend's polite face, knock him to the ground and then kick him while he lay between the chairs on the stone terrace. Instead, he walked away a few feet, as though he were thinking this through. Gave himself time, just enough, to turn, smiling, and reply, with a reassuring hand on Gerald's shoulder, 'Well, thank you, I can assure you there's nothing going on, I know her well enough for that, but thank you all the same.'

In his head he saw Zelda and Edouard laughing under the almond tree, her hand on his thigh, and he heard the reproof in Gerald's voice and winced as much for his own guilt as for hers. He went into the house.

That night, tossing and turning in the sultry heat, he ordered Zelda never to see Josanne again, never to let the Frenchmen into the house, never to talk to them on the beach. She argued at first – not her innocence but her justification, her misery, his desertion, his lack of understanding of her position. All the time he saw Zelda and Josanne under the tree and Sara watching him, from behind a half-open door.

Next day he wondered, seriously, if he would ever get over it; if Zelda had so damaged their marriage that it could never be reclaimed. It had been, for him, something almost holy, and he recalled those mornings at mass when he was a boy, the smell of incense, the ringing bell and the miracle of the body and the blood. Now it was smashed, like the china and glasses he broke when he was drunk. He swirled the Bushmills in his glass. Where had that devout boy gone? And what had become of the promising writer? Normally, Scott tried hard not to drink when he was writing, but now he needed the comfort of alcohol too much for self-discipline. Without it, he would go under; without it, he would never be able to finish his book.

Somehow, despite his emotional turmoil and his drinking, he kept up the good work on *Gatsby*. His relief at being able to write properly again should have been joyful, but was now tarnished by strains of guilt, that he had bought his success at the expense of Zelda's happiness – wasn't that what the Murphys had thought? Wasn't that partly true?

By August 1924 he was so close to finishing the book that he could afford time away from his desk, so they took days out together and drove over to Antibes to visit the Murphys on the beach at La Garoupe. This became the first summer season, as it would later be known, on the Riviera. At Antibes they joined Picasso, with his wife, his son, Paulo, and his mother, wrapped in her black Spanish clothes. Cole Porter, a university friend of Scott's, had taken a château nearby and came over with his wife to join the Murphys and their friends. John dos Passos and fellow

American writer Archibald MacLeish and their wives were staying at the hotel (Ernest Hemingway would come later), and the
French cabaret star Mistinguett (partner of Maurice Chevalier)
was another guest of Gerald and Sara's. There were dogs and
children (including Paulo Picasso and the young Murphys) for
Scottie to play with and everyone − children, grown-ups and
granny − lived outside on the beach, under parasols and umbrellas, while Gerald, with whatever assistance he could muster,
painstakingly raked away seaweed to reveal virgin sand.

Beneath the shade of her parasol, Scott sat with Sara and
watched Zelda lying on a bamboo mat in the sun. Later, Zelda went
for a swim, and Scott knew the others were watching and admiring
the strength of her stroke. He thought of her legs and watched a
powder of sand on Sara's thighs. The whole of his world seemed
to have been condensed into this place and this moment: the heat,
the white light, nearly bled of colour and, on this empty coast, in a
deserted land, just this group of people, concentrating all human
life into the filtered sunlight of those umbrellas.[28] By midday, even
the white line five miles away that was Cannes had disappeared,
and their world had been reduced to a solitary boat that seemed to
be pulling behind it a strand of the deeper, darker sea.[29]

In the hotel at lunchtime, the empty dining room was cool
and chequered with the shadows of the pines outside.

'I fell in love on the beach,' Zelda said to Gerald.

To Scott, the chequered shadows swayed perilously over the
white tablecloths like a boat rocking at sea, but it was only
the motion of the pines.[30]

In the afternoon, he went for a drive along the coast as far as Monte Carlo. The sea was changing its colours, green as green milk, blue as laundry water, wine dark, and as the heat went out of the day, people came outside to eat in front of their houses. When he turned the car off the corniche and headed down to the Cap through the darkening banks of trees, the moon was out, hovering over the ruins of the aqueduct. There was a faint sound of music carried from a party somewhere in the hills behind the hotel and he felt both a sense of goodwill to all men and an opposing tightening in his stomach towards Zelda and Sara.[31]

They drank cocktails before dinner, while the children had their baths. Gerald mixed the drinks while the waiters looked on in admiration or condescension – Scott was not sure which. The waiters were Italian and spoke to each other in musical sentences, which made Scott think of the mass, and Gerald was like a priest, seriously caught up in the ritual of glasses and shakers.

Zelda began to dance, drawing Dos Passos into an embrace, humming and extemporising the tune. They danced well and the others clapped. At dinner she hardly ate.

'But don't you find the seaside so boring?' she asked Sara.

Suddenly, as though she could put up with them no longer, she got up and ran outside, discarding her evening clothes as she climbed the rocky headland of the Cap. The sun was setting, turning the sky marble pink; against the grey rock they could see her climbing upwards. Scott, with a terrible understanding of what she was going to do, got up and ran after her, following her

102

up the cliffs and on to the grassy summit, where Zelda turned to face him, her face ecstatic, her eyes bright.

'Isn't this just the most wonderful place in the world? After this, nothing else can matter!'

And as the startled diners watched, she dived, gracefully, straight into the blackness of the rock-strewn sea. Scott closed his eyes and jumped into the void, then he was deep under water but alive and unhurt, and then, with Zelda, swimming through dark silk towards the shore.

'Wasn't that just wonderful, Scott! Let's just keep swimming and never, never go back.'

Others had come down to the water's edge, anxiously peering out into the blackness. They applauded when they saw them swim to shore.

Ada MacLeish said, 'Oh Zelda, what a shock you gave us!'

And Sara, angry, added, 'How could you? You might have killed yourself and Scott.'

In the silence, Zelda, shining, said, 'But Say-ra, don't you know? We don't believe in conservation.'

On the drive home together they laughed, at the adventure and at the Murphys.

'There is something about them,' Zelda started.

Scott agreed. 'I know just what you mean.'

'Something that makes me want to shock them, to smash their nursery-like peace and goodwill to all men.'

'And that constant emphasis on the simpler virtues,'[32] added Scott.

Sharing their insights made them feel close, closer than they had for ages.

'It was fun playing chicken, wasn't it?'

They played chicken all the time: Zelda daring Scott to ever greater risks, forcing him to take his hands off the steering wheel at the most dangerous bend on the coast road to light her ciga-rette; making him drive over her, as she lay in the road in front of the car. Even without him, Zelda would play chicken, driving her car off the road so that it hung over the sea, climbing alone in the dark over the stony hillside at the back of their house, searching for ruined abbeys and fallen churches.

Scott played chicken with Sara, too, but she did not know she was playing. Sometimes his need to be with her was so strong that he had to get her to acknowledge him. Like a schoolboy he would stare at her, brazen, hostile, daring her to return his stare, her bright blue eyes on him alone. This too Zelda understood; it was part of the challenge of the Murphys, their distance, despite their openness. There was never any intimacy, any real nakedness; it was all, somehow, meticulously staged and played out for the audience's benefit. When he was drunk, Scott tried to smash through the polished veneer and go backstage. He wanted to find their friends engaged in something shocking: cannibalism – that would do, he and Zelda laughed. That was why he tried to shock them, to get them to show themselves as they really were.

Then one evening when they had drunk more than usual, and were too tired to drive home, they agreed to stay in the

104

hotel. Zelda told Scott she had taken an overdose; she lay half-conscious on the bed, her speech slurred and her eyes closed.

'Get the Murphys,' she told him. 'They will know what to do.'

All night, patient Sara and Gerald kept Zelda awake, walking her up and down the tortuous corridor of the hotel. Sometimes Sara let Gerald sleep for an hour, whispering to him to go and she would take care of Zelda alone. Then Zelda staggered, gripping Sara tighter.

'My husband is in love with you, you know, he thinks you are divine.'

Gerald was patient and protective.

'You have a loving husband and a wonderful daughter. You have friends and family, what can have made you want to do this?'

'Oh Gerald, if you only knew,' groaned Zelda, 'if you knew what was really going on.'

In the morning, driving home together, she told Scott and they laughed.

'Why do we do things like that to them?'

'It's partly because we like them so much, isn't it?'

'And partly because we can't stand them.'

As the summer came to a close, the Murphy party dispersed; Scott's novel was completed and the manuscript on its way to his publisher in New York. *The Great Gatsby* was published in autumn 1925 to huge literary acclaim, confirming Scott as a 'real writer' and building and expanding his reputation.

With the fulfilment of his dream, to be recognised as a literary as well as a popular writer, came the expected anticlimax.

Once again Scott was riding high, rich on royalties, writing the frothy pieces demanded by the *Post*, which brought in even more money. Paris had become the New York scene they had fled; Fitzgerald was drinking heavily and partying. That winter in Paris was 'the time of a thousand parties and no work'.[33] As Gertrude Stein said: 'Paris was where all Europe was.'

And the Fitzgeralds had to be at its centre as they partied with Cole Porter and Josephine Baker; met Diaghilev and attended the first night of Cocteau and Stravinsky's *Oedipus Rex*. Hemingway, with his second wife, Pauline, was a neighbour, as were the American modernist writers ee cummings and John dos Passos.

Under the strain of this socialising, Fitzgerald's drinking and Zelda's psychological problems, the marriage was falling apart. By contrast, Fitzgerald became obsessed with the Murphys' relationship, asking them highly personal questions on their sex lives before and during marriage, and subjecting Gerald to a catechism of questions on, for example, the design of his bag: 'What is that bag you are carrying? Where did you buy it? What is it called? Is it your design? Why all the straps and buckles, Gerald, are you some sort of fetishist?'

Gerald was too polite to rebuff his friend, but Sara was more outspoken, telling him in a letter that while their friendship was not in doubt:

> …you can't expect anyone to like or stand a Continual feeling of analysis & subanalysis & criticism…
>
> Letter from SWM to FSF, 1926

Scott's infatuation with the Murphys grew, whether out of love for Sara or hero worship of Gerald. He stalked Gerald across Paris and lay in wait for him at his bank; he asked him personal questions about his marriage. In some ways he was researching a character for his novel, but the intrusion went much further. In effect, he wanted to merge their identities (as he does in his next novel), to become Gerald, married to Sara. Disruptive, abusive and highly offensive, a drunk Fitzgerald would wake the Murphys in the early hours and demand to be let in to the house, living out his fantasy in awful intoxicated reality.

The Murphys were worried about Fitzgerald, but even more concerned about Zelda and the effect of his behaviour on her. Zelda had returned from their trip to America slightly nearer to the edge than before. In the States she had taken up dancing, and now wanted to pursue her hobby with professional training in Paris. She turned for help to Gerald, who knew all the members of the Ballets Russes. Disturbed by his feelings that Zelda was too old for a career in ballet, Gerald felt that if he did not help her, she would somehow break down. He therefore introduced her to a teacher, with whom Zelda had lessons. Her classes began to take over her life: obsessive, not eating and terrified of being too old, Zelda became entirely caught up in her new pastime. Her performances were embarrassing and largely ignored by Fitzgerald, lost in his own fantasy. Sara accused him of not knowing anything about the life of Zelda or their daughter, Scottie. But life continued as before – unable to work because of his drinking, Fitzgerald drank more and Zelda tried to dance herself into oblivion.

The world was changing; the Murphys had noticed it the previous summer on the beach at Antibes where money, celebrity and vulgarity were beginning to invade the innocent world they had created.

What had been simple and sophisticated was turning rotten and self-indulgent. Something was 'rotting like water lilies among the massed pines and the rose tinted paintwork of the hotel now seemed almost feverish and flushed, bloated perhaps by heat and indulgence'.[34]

The news from home was violent, too: the tinsel years of the Roaring Twenties were beginning to break down or blow up in ways that Scott found particularly upsetting. A Princeton classmate killed himself and his wife; friends in Philadelphia and New York jumped to their deaths from skyscrapers; in Chicago, a friend was murdered in a speakeasy, and on the hallowed ground of the Princeton Club a friend died from a beating administered in a bar.[35]

Meanwhile, the Murphys' new villa in the hills behind Antibes was finished and they moved into it for the summer. Villa America, their own home was, of course, a work of art. Designed by Gerald, whose decorative house sign typified the blend of French and American influences, it was a stunning mix of American 1920s' black and white tiles and aluminium furniture set against the Provençal charm of stone-walled terraces on the rocky hillside, dotted with grey olives and dark cypresses.

The summer of 1925 began, like all such disasters, slowly and harmlessly enough. *The Great Gatsby* had been published in the States in April to great acclaim. The Fitzgeralds were in Juan-les-Pins and the Murphys nearby in the Villa America, the house they had designed and built. But the place where they swam was now 'a club', though, like the international society it represented, it would be hard to say who was not admitted.[36] The beach grew crowded with chic society girls and older men, but no one swam any more from the rocks on the Cap or raked the seaweed from the pale yellow sand. Scott and Zelda were drinking again, and Scott's writing was not going smoothly. In the evenings they would walk across the Pinède to the dusty casino on the other side of the small square. There would be violence – nothing very serious, just Scott throwing ashtrays, insulting fellow drinkers and getting into fights. The next day he would be full of his seductive charm – there were apologies and excuses and he would pay for the damage and make up with Zelda.

At the Murphys some evenings there were parties, immortalised in what would be Fitzgerald's last completed novel, *Tender is the Night* (1934). The Murphys had a rare gift for entertaining – not the conventional showy productions or 'holocausts', as Sara called them, but wonderfully original, intimate occasions built round their family and their friends and bringing everyone into the special warmth of the Murphys' own good fortune. The parties started with the children, washed and dressed for bed, performing a song or play in the gardens. They were creative, gifted children, and often Gerald or Sara took part too, dressing up and acting or playing an instrument without embarrassment. Then, when the children had gone to bed and the sky was turning pale, there would be cocktails on the terrace below the house. Gerald took as much care with these as with everything he did, creating his own recipes, mixing them so carefully they became almost ritualistic. As the huge moon rose from the horizon, turning the sea silver, the party got under way. There were candlelit tables, which Sara had decorated with flowers or toys or whatever else took her fancy; there was the sweet scent of honeysuckle and roses, while from the distant trees the song of nightingales blended with the 'ghostly wash of the Mediterranean far below'.[37] Everything woven together by their brilliant hosts to create something like a spell, which lifted the guests and transported them to their best selves – more witty, more beautiful and definitely more loveable than when they had arrived.[38]

The serpents in this paradise were Scott and Zelda. Denied their rightful place as the absolute centre of attention, they began behaving badly in order to attract the notice they craved. One evening, Scott disgraced himself by throwing figs at the temptingly bare back of a French dowager. Another time he smashed his hosts' Venetian glasses on the rocks of the hillside behind the house. When the Murphys sent Archie MacLeish to remonstrate with him, Scott turned on the messenger and became so aggressive that a fight ensued in which he, Scott, was knocked out cold. The pattern was tedious and unchanging: in the mornings, contrite and charming, Scott would feign no recollection of what he had done and blame his drinking, for which he took no responsibility. When the Murphys banned him from their house for three weeks, he accepted with good grace, but on his return continued to behave as before.

In Zelda's case, it was her terrible recklessness that was so unsettling. One evening, when the Murphys and Fitzgeralds were dining together on the terrace of the Colombe d'Or in Saint-Paul de Vence, Scott noticed the dancer Isadora Duncan, now retired, at a nearby table and went over to pay his respects. He stayed away so long that Zelda grew bored and, in a petulant fit, got up and strode over to the wall that surrounded the terrace and protected guests from the perilous drop down to the hill below. As the stunned diners watched her, she threw herself over the edge of the wall. The Murphys expected to find her mangled remains in the olive groves hundreds of feet below, but she was, of course, unharmed and calmly walking up a flight of stone steps leading from the hillside back to the restaurant. Another evening, in the casino at Juan, she began to dance on the table, providing the French locals with a shocking spectacle as she lifted her skirt above her waist and, eyes closed, swayed seductively to the music. It was, their friends agreed afterwards, her oblivion that was the most distressing part of the experience.

Zelda had always been unpredictable, but her behaviour had at least been held within the bounds of propriety. Now, however, she was straying beyond the boundaries into strange new territory, taking risks she was no longer sharp enough to manage and exposing herself in ways that suggested an inner turmoil. She was rude to friends and strangers, letting rip her acerbic tongue, heedless of the offence she was likely to cause.

'I hope you die in the marble ring,' she whispered under her breath semi-audibly as she graciously greeted another diner who had recognised her. This was apparently a schoolgirl curse but, even if incomprehensible, its deeper meaning was clearly unflattering and antisocial.

Back in Paris, Zelda continued her extreme dance training. She was acutely aware of her age and worked twice as hard as her younger colleagues to compensate for her handicap. Her dance routine was punishing: she went to classes in the morning and afternoon and set herself an exacting practice regime. She hardly ate and obsessively measured herself and her progress against her fellow students.

Eventually, Zelda collapsed and was admitted first to a medical and then to a mental hospital. Fitzgerald moved her to a clinic in Switzerland, where the doctors were amazingly insightful and sensitive, spotting that many of her problems stemmed from her marriage to a successful figure. Scott was ordered to stop his drinking and was not allowed to visit Zelda for a while. Doubtless this added to his feelings of guilt and self-reproach, and he was most loyal and attentive when he was allowed to visit her again.

Sadly, the Murphys too were in Switzerland because of the tragic illness of their son Patrick, who had been diagnosed with TB. Brave even under this terrible sentence, the Murphys had moved to Crans-Montana and had bought a small restaurant, where they held parties with music and food every weekend.

The great novel that centres around Dick and Nicole Diver was inspired by the Murphys and Fitzgerald's obsession with them. In part, writing the book enabled him to 'be' the Murphys, Scott and Zelda become Dick and Nicole Diver. It took him nine years to write. By that time, the lives of the Fitzgeralds and Murphys had been totally shattered, but the spell of those magical parties and of their delicious friendship was captured for ever against the background of an innocent Riviera.

Tender is the Night is one of the most moving love stories ever written, as well as being a powerful elegy to the Riviera golden years and to post First World War America. Fitzgerald managed to convey both his love of the Côte d'Azur and his awareness of its dangers; it is this sense of doom that makes the novel so unsettling. On the one hand there is the stunning beauty of the scenes, the sensuous mingling of smell, sight and sound that is sometimes almost too perfect to bear (Keats' poem, from which the title of the novel is taken, is, after all, about committing suicide). In the detail of his descriptions, he captures the beauty of the colour and light of the Riviera, almost like an Impressionist painting: the tan prayer mat of sand outside the hotel, the purple of the mountains in the distance and the white flatness of the sky at midday evoke the South of France for ever. Yet he also shows us its other side, for his novel is one of destruction and despair, of the breakdown of a marriage and a man and of the unsustainability of the Riviera dream.

ALDOUS HUXLEY

It was the dying D.H. Lawrence who brought Aldous Huxley to the South of France in 1930. Lawrence had moved to the Riviera, hoping, like his friend Katherine Mansfield, that the warmth would cure his TB. But, like her, he would find himself bitterly disappointed. Finally, and against his wishes, his wife, Frieda, had to move him to a sanatorium in Vence, where Aldous and Maria Huxley came to visit him. As good friends, they helped Frieda to fulfil his last wish and move him home to die, where they shared the nursing, sitting patiently by his bedside until his peaceful death.

The friendship between Lawrence and Huxley was unexpected. The two giants of literature came from opposite ends of the social spectrum – Lawrence, the working-class provincial, was the son of a semi-literate father, while Huxley came from the intellectual elite. His grandfather, T.H. Huxley, was a friend and collaborator of Charles Darwin and a famous supporter of the claims of science over religion. While Lawrence was a romantic who glorified in man's feelings and emotions, Huxley prided himself on his understanding of science and took great pride in his rationality. This could often appear as coldness on Huxley's part, and indeed Lawrence had himself told Frieda that he found the Huxleys distant and cold.

In reality, nothing could have been further from the truth, as the Huxleys showed in their actions during and after Lawrence's death. They stayed on to support Frieda at the Hôtel Beau Rivage at Bandol, where Aldous started sorting through Lawrence's papers, and the couple helped Frieda arrange his funeral. Almost unexpectedly, they found themselves viewing the area as a possible place to live and, to their own surprise, found a house in nearby Sanary, a tiny fishing village just along the coast. As Maria wrote to a friend, it 'is nothing that I wanted except the position – in the country & two minutes from good bathing…' (letter to Mary Hutchinson, 10 March 1930).

Aldous hated the built-up area of the Riviera proper, along the coast between Menton and Cannes – 'The whole thing is one vast and sordid suburb, the suburb of all Europe' (letter to Julian Huxley, 3 March 1930) – but in Sanary he found an unspoiled innocence that surprised and pleased him. Steeped as they were in the immediate grief of losing a good friend, the house and its wonderful gardens, stocked with vines, figs and olives, must have seemed like a welcome antidote. What the villa lacked in beauty, it made up for in convenience – as Maria said, it was close to the sea and it had mains water. As an added attraction, the impatient Huxleys and their young son, Matthew, could move in almost straightaway. The Huxleys were always impulsive; now they threw themselves into the Sanary project, employing builders to substantially remodel the villa to their needs but enjoying it even when the house was torn apart, as Huxley wrote to his sister-in-law:

> Here all is exquisitely lovely, sun, roses, fruit, warmth. We
> bathe and bask. Best love to all.
>
> 31 May 1930

The area around Bandol and Sanary was, in those days, still undiscovered and quite un-smart, so the remodelling of the house was not the extravagance it might seem. Indeed, Huxley was always careful about money (advising his friend T.S. Eliot, for example, to come down on the third-class sleeper) but was generous in supporting friends in need. Although he probably had a comfortable nest egg of private means in the background, he preferred to live as simply as possible: Sybille Bedford, the Huxleys' young neighbour, friend and eventual biographer of Huxley, described the village of Sanary as she found it when she moved there with her mother, a few years before the Huxleys arrived:

> Sanary in 1926, like Cassis, like Bandol, had about half
> a dozen small hotels, some pensions, a score or two of
> (unheatable) villas for summer letting – were there a hundred
> who came for the quatorze juillet and August? A hundred
> and fifty? The permanent local population was about two
> thousand according to the Michelin of the time...[39]

The local people were traditional French peasant farmers and fishermen served by a few artisans.

> In the decades of innocence the inhabitants lived mostly off each other and the export of vegetables, flowers and fine fish. They were cultivateurs, fishermen, shopkeepers, a doctor or two, the notaire, the pharmacien, the postmistress, the schoolmistress, the retired naval officer sustained by opium and his books, the stray Scandinavian artist.[40]

The Huxleys had always loved the Italian Mediterranean but had left Italy because of the growth of fascism. Now they could enjoy the sea again in an area that appeared almost idyllically unspoiled and natural. For Huxley, whose eyesight was a major medical problem, the clear light of the Riviera must also have been a blessing. Huxley wrote every day but rationed the amount of work he gave to his eyes very strictly so as not to wear them out reading anything but the most important material. This discipline extended to the typing of his manuscripts, which was carried out by Maria, who also read to him and acted as his chauffeur.

The Huxleys were an immensely hospitable couple and typically had their house full of guests every year for the long summers. Friends remembered the Mediterranean informality of the villa – the terracotta-tiled living-room floor, scattered with Mexican rugs and scented with the delicate exotic aroma of Maria's pot pourri, mixed from the herbs she grew in her vegetable garden. Yet, for all the bohemianism, there was a balancing practicality – the villa had good plumbing, ample hot water and, in the winter, central heating. Friends noticed the calm and orderliness of the home, which was important for Huxley's writing and enforced by Maria when the house was full of visitors.

Under contract to produce two books a year, Huxley wrote 500–700 words after breakfast every morning, while his house guests played on the beach. He was also trying to publish a collection of Lawrence's letters, with contributions from many of his friends, as well as writing his own non-fiction and answering copious correspondence. At noon he would emerge, stooping and blinking in the bright light, from his garden study and join his house guests for a swim in the sea. Aldous and Maria both wore the same outfit: white canvas sailor's trousers, bought in Marseilles, and a coolie-type hat, which Aldous even kept on when he went swimming. He would swim next to Maria, keeping up a strong breaststroke as he told her what he had achieved that morning and discussed the next day's writing. Lunch was back at the house in the reflected light of the mirrored dining room. Huxley was a charming host, talking easily with everyone. In the afternoons, he painted (his works decorated the house), dealt with his post and read the newspaper until teatime – Earl Grey and ginger biscuits – when he would retire to write again. Meanwhile, Maria typed his manuscripts, worked in the garden or entertained the guests with walks and trips to the beach, where they might be joined again by Huxley for a late swim before dinner in the delicious cool of the day.

Moonless, this June night is all the more alive with stars. Its darkness is perfumed with faint gusts from the blossoming lime trees, with the smell of wetted earth and the invisible greenness of the vines. There is silence; but a silence that breathes with the soft breathing of the sea and, in the thin shrill noise of a cricket, ... Far away, the passage of a train...[41]

A visit to the Huxleys was not simply about sensuous pleasures, for Aldous – by now one of the greatest intellects of his time – was also very good company and enjoyed the company of other interesting minds. Despite his poor eyesight, he was exceptionally well read and could converse in an informed manner on an enormous range of topics that included medicine, musicology, theology, chemistry, poetry, classical literature and modern physics. The evenings were always busy with talk of the latest books and theories. During the day there would be interesting projects, such as photographing insects, and the guests, young or old, were charmed by Huxley's ease and charm. Edith Wharton, who lived nearby and was by then an elderly lady, was struck by his company, describing him as:

Human, conversible, full of fun and eminently sociable.

Letter to John Hugh Smith, 1930

The intergenerational friendship was clearly strong and when the Huxleys planned to leave France, Wharton wrote to her friend Berenson:

They will be a great loss to me, as they supply the only real talk I get, except for my guests.

Letter to Bernard Berenson, 1937

The Huxleys' friend Sybille Bedford shed a witty light on the relationship when she remembered Huxley once guiding Wharton down some steep stairs in his villa and…

…patting Mrs Wharton's behind. The entourage froze; Mrs Wharton turned her head, not abruptly … and gave him a sweet smile.[42]

It was, however, often hard to keep him entertained and stimulated, especially in the off-season spells with fewer visitors, when Aldous hankered for the social life and libraries of London. Staying in France was his best way of earning enough to live on without having to resort to magazine journalism, but it came at a price.

Meanwhile, to their guests he and Maria seemed like the perfect couple:

Maria so exquisite, always deliciously scented, wearing lovely silks and furs, gardenias and coral ear-rings, and doing the craziest exercises on her bed room floor…

Sophie Welling, née Moulaert (niece of Aldous and Maria Huxley), to Sybille Bedford for inclusion in her biography of Huxley (see note 41 for details)

In 1930, editing Lawrence's letters for publication as he had promised, Huxley came back to England and visited the Nottinghamshire mining village where D.H. Lawrence had grown up. The visit introduced him to the lives of the industrialised British working class, an experience that both shocked and angered him. Characteristically, Huxley's anger combined an unattractive criticism of the lives of working men with an attack on himself and his own (class) ignorance of the conditions in which so much of England lived. Travelling north from Nottingham to Durham to address a miners' adult education class, he had a similar experience; and staying with his friend the Dean in the confines of the Cathedral Close, he discovered again a near total ignorance among the upper classes of the lives and struggles of the poor living only a few miles away. Having had his eyes opened to the segregation of English social and occupational life, Huxley wrote about it in a piece entitled 'Abroad in England',[43] which captured the distance and lack of understanding between the classes and the enormity of the geographical north/south divide.

It was these visits, and the contrasts he found between British (industrial) and French (rural) lifestyles, that culminated in the creation of his best-known novel, *Brave New World*, which he wrote in Sanary-sur-Mer in 1931.

In a letter of May 1931, he described the novel in progress: 'I am writing a novel about the future – on the horror of the Wellsian Utopia and a revolt against it.'

By August, he could write to his father:

I have been harried by work – which I have at last got rid of:-
a comic, or at least satirical, novel about the Future, showing
that apallingness *[sic]* (at any rate by our standards) of Utopia
and adumbrating the effects on thought and feeling of such
quite possible biological interventions as the production
of children in bottles, (with consequent abolition of the
family and all the Freudian 'Complexes' for which family
relationships are responsible, the prolongation of youth, the
devising of some harmless but effective substitute for alcohol,
cocaine, opium etc:- and also the effects of such sociological
reforms as Pavlovian conditioning of all children from birth
and before birth, universal peace, security and stability).

The anger and pessimism of the novel can be broken down into
two major themes, and although the first of the two – genetic
engineering or eugenics – was the theme that first captured the
popular imagination, it is the second – consumerism and its link
with mass production – that strikes one today as the most keenly
prescient. In the world that Huxley imagines, human suffering has been eradicated through advances in science. Poverty,
hunger and disease are no longer threatening giants. They have
been eliminated by state-run breeding plants, which carefully
control the type and number of people created and match them
closely to the needs of the workforce, keeping them fed, healthy
and happy through artificial means. Sexual relations are purely
acts of pleasure, not procreation, and conventional units like
the family have ceased to exist. Conditioned from birth, the

population accepts its own passivity and slavery willingly, dulled by a continual desire to consume that keeps it compliant and the machinery of mass production rolling.

Huxley had read Henry Ford's philosophy and observed at first hand the real advances achieved through mass production. He was, however, also keenly aware of the 'downside' to mass production and consumerism in terms of overpopulation and pollution. In the novel he takes his analysis many stages further and explores the coarsening effect of materialism, the loss of an essential element of humanity destroyed through the 'anomie' of industrialisation and, in moral terms, an encroaching passivity and concomitant loss of free will. It is a massive and highly depressing dystopian theme, which at its heart attacks Huxley's sacred cow of scientific progress. Written under a terrible wave of anger and despair, it is perhaps only right that it should have been created in a rural paradise, as far away as possible from the over-populated industrial world Huxley imagined. No longer living in Britain allowed Huxley to feel all the more keenly its foreignness or 'alienation', as he described it in a subsequent interview:

The England that I thought I knew has so completely changed, that, for me, it has become a strange country. I can make nothing of it; the harsh music, the blatant vulgarity, the Talkies...[44]

He was also horrified by a visit to the United States, where he had encountered mass consumerism and group mentality.

Brave New World was published to great success in Britain early in 1932, but the Huxleys stayed in France. It was usually their custom to celebrate the publication of a book by taking a short sightseeing break. When they were living in Italy, this had involved an immersion in art, visiting churches and galleries. In France, Huxley complained, this was not possible. Instead he, Maria, Sybille Bedford and a young blonde girl went to Cannes in the Huxley Bugatti. The Huxleys had dinner with H.G. Wells, whose science-fiction novels had undoubtedly inspired Huxley's *Brave New World*. Wells was collaborating with Huxley's brother Julian on a forthcoming scientific publication and had other family links (as a young student at night school, he had studied under the great T.H. Huxley), but Aldous' opinion of him echoed the Bloomsbury set's snobbishly damning verdict that he was a rather vulgar writer.

There were, it appears, two sides to Huxley: there was the Aldous Huxley who was a charming host and brilliant conversationalist and the man who created the destructive dark vision of *Brave New World*, the dystopian masterpiece. Was there something troubled and insecure beneath the charming veneer?

There was a cold distance about Huxley, noted not only by the Lawrences but probably by other friends who received his many letters from France. His letters rarely reveal anything of the real man and never deal with feelings or emotions. Carefully worded, courteous and pleasant in tone, even his family missives are dry and unrevealing. For example, his stay in France involves only seeing his son, Matthew, in the holidays; meeting him again after absences, he focuses on an analysis of Matthew's appearance rather than any display of his own feelings for his son or his son's emotional development.

> Mentally he is the image of M's family – quick, with a remarkable intuitive power for grasping the essentials of a situation, a natural gift for living; but with a quite unusual incapacity to grasp and apply general principles – which is rather deplorable if he wants to embrace any of the more learned professions.
>
> Aldous Huxley to Leonard Huxley, 12 September 1932

An even more shocking lack of emotion is recorded in his reaction to the arrival in Sanary of refugee writers fleeing Hitler.

> Swarms of literary Germans infest the countryside like locusts.
>
> Aldous Huxley to Ottoline Morrell, 1931

and

> Sanary swarms with German literary exiles, from Thomas Mann downwards. The place fairly stinks of literature – which is rather distressing.
>
> Aldous Huxley to Eugene Saxton, 1933

Although the writing is offensive, it perhaps reveals a deep-seated fear of emotion and its expression. Early in his life, Aldous had been struck by three terrible tragedies. First, his mother had died suddenly when he was thirteen. The unexpected news came to him when he was innocently caught up in school affairs at Eton and was looking forward to his brothers' visit for the famous annual Wall Game. Thirty years later, he described the long-lasting effects of a similar trauma on one of his characters:

> There remained with him, latent at ordinary times but always ready to come to the surface, a haunting sense of the vanity, the transience, the hopeless precariousness of all merely human happiness.[45]

This could be a very fine description of himself.

Huxley lost his beloved mother and, with her, the security of his childhood. Until then the family had lived happily in (unspoiled) Surrey, where Aldous had enjoyed an Arcadian childhood playing for hours in the woods, discovering rare flowers and insects. When his mother died, the house, which was also her school, was sold and Huxley's father moved to bachelor accommodation in London. The older boys were already at Oxford and may have had friends to visit in the holidays, while Aldous and his sister were passed between relatives. The family, the house and his mother had all disappeared.

A couple of years later, he tragically lost his sight and became almost blind. Unable to continue at school, he was sent home to live in an isolated, dark world where he could no longer indulge in his favourite occupation – reading. Seemingly undaunted,

Huxley taught himself Braille so that he could access books; played the piano daily; and with sheer self-discipline and lack of self-pity resumed his studies with a private tutor. When his eyesight returned and he was able to sit the Balliol College exams at Oxford (with a magnifying glass), he not only gained a place but had caught up with his contemporaries and went up with his cousin Gervas, who was his age. One can only imagine the longer-term effect of this sudden calamity and the lessons of self-reliance and mistrust of others that it taught him. To be doubly alone in a dark world by the age of eighteen must have left deep scars.

Meanwhile, Huxley senior remarried – a woman younger than Aldous' older brothers, and though Aldous eventually got on well with Rosalind, he must initially have been threatened by her presence and what it signified. One of the consequences of his father's new life was that Aldous turned towards his brother Trevenen, who was, like him, at Balliol, although in his last year of a postgraduate degree. The brothers got on well and in January 1913 went on a walking holiday together. Aldous spent part of the following spring and summer vacations living with his brother at Trev's digs in Oxford. Trev, who was in many ways the easiest and most likeable of the Huxley brothers, was a troubled young man. Overwhelmed by his failure to gain a First in his Finals, he was now involved with a young woman of the wrong class, whom he knew would never be accepted by the Huxley family. In this mood, he failed the Civil Service entrance exams and suffered a nervous breakdown. Trev went to the hospital that had successfully treated the oldest brother, Julian, the summer before, but this time the outcome was tragic. Young Trev committed suicide and was found after eight terrible days of searching, having hanged himself from a tree.

Each tragedy alone would have sown seeds of bitterness and mistrust, an emphasis on self-reliance and an isolation that made relationships difficult. Huxley's self-awareness is shown in his early characters such as Stone in *Crome Yellow* (1921) and Walter Bidlake in *Point Counter Point* (1928), who are clearly autobiographical; both suffer shame that they cannot really get on with other people, especially the common man, and in the latter novel Huxley writes a moving description of an early childhood memory involving Bidlake's mother and the smell of a sickroom interspersed with a contemporary repulsion at the smell of a working-class companion. Subconsciously and revealingly, this inability to relate to other people is linked with the loss of his mother. At a later date, Huxley wrote to a friend, 'I share with you a fear of the responsibilities of relationships – have only one that really counts at all, with my wife – nothing else that commits me in any serious way.' (letter to Flora Strousse, 19 February 1932). Although his relationship with Maria was strong and she was the devoted wife, secretary, chauffeur, mother and hostess she appeared, she was also much more. She too had had a troubled past: coming to England from bourgeois Belgium as a young refugee because of the German invasion, it was Maria's good fortune to have been offered accommodation by Lady Ottoline Morrell at Garsington, her famous Elizabethan manor outside Oxford,

an oasis for artists and intellectuals of the day. Ottoline and Philip
Morrell were outstandingly generous hosts, but for the sixteen-
year-old, French-speaking Maria it was a heady but disturbing
contrast with her sheltered bourgeois Belgian background. Later
in life she admitted that she had been very unhappy there. Unsure
and insecure, she became infatuated with Ottoline Morrell with
serious results that involved a suicide attempt when she thought
they might be separated. No less a person than D.H. Lawrence
argued with Ottoline on her behalf, accusing the hostess of being
controlling and domineering to a naive and inexperienced girl.
Although Maria appeared to recover, she continued to be deeply
in love with Ottoline and emotionally dependent on her even
when she had met Huxley, who was at first a guest and then a
fellow lodger at Garsington, where he worked on the estate farm.

Maria's sexuality was not straightforward: she had affairs
with many women, some of whom were also sleeping with
Aldous, who had frequent affairs himself. This aspect of their
married life was not unusual in Bloomsbury circles, but may have
given an additional strain (as well as frisson) to their relationship.
Importantly, there was no deception in this open marriage, and
when Maria felt that her husband's affair with Nancy Cunard
was entering dangerous waters, she delivered the ultimatum that
led the Huxleys to leave England for Italy. Their three-way affair
with Mary Hutchinson was more evenly reciprocated, with both
Aldous and Maria openly having Mary as a lover.

In a letter to Mary from Italy, Maria talks of their time
together in bed in Oxford and then adds, 'Aldous knows I am

writing and pays you devoted court and wishes to be allowed to kiss your hand hoping you forgave him long ago for discovering his character not to be frivolous and naughty.' On another occasion Maria wrote to Mary, 'Aldous has just come into my bed and he smelt so strongly of you still that it made one giddy.' Despite, or perhaps because of, their open affairs, the Huxley marriage was a strong and supportive one, but their frequent illnesses reveal something of the strains they were under. These strains, especially on Huxley's side, became ever more apparent in his writing.

In Huxley's first novel, *Crome Yellow*, a huge literary success, he describes with witty sarcasm life in a thinly disguised Garsington. Huxley had received nothing but generosity from the Morrells, who had introduced him to artistic society and provided him with a substitute home where he could meet and converse with like-minded, intelligent people. When he left for London, he wrote sincerely that his time there had been 'the happiest time in my life' (letter to Philip and Ottoline Morrell, undated). He went on to tell them how much he had received from them without being able to repay, 'Unless a very deep devotion counts at all in the balance against your gifts of inspiration, almost creation.'

Such gratitude, however, didn't prevent Huxley from the ultimate betrayal, which was to pen in *Crome Yellow* a cruel caricature of Ottoline, thinly disguised as Priscilla Wimbush, and of Garsington and its guests. Priscilla had:

> …a large square middle-aged face, with a massive projecting nose and little greenish eyes, the whole surmounted by a

lofty and elaborate coiffure of a curiously improbable shade of orange.[46]

Ottoline was very deeply hurt, both for herself and for the guests whom he had similarly caricatured in the novel. Writing to Ottoline, Huxley replied disingenuously that he had not intended anyone to read his characters as real people or their setting as Garsington, and then added,

> This incident is to me another proof of something I said in the book: we are all parallel straight lines destined to meet only at infinity. Real understanding is an impossibility.
>
> 3 December 1921

Huxley's next novel, *Point Counter Point*, was another attack on society, especially artistic and intellectual society. Although, like *Crome Yellow*, it was a *roman-à-clef* with easily recognisable sources such as the artist Augustus John, the critic John Middleton Murry and the author D.H. Lawrence as thinly disguised characters, he managed the balance between wit and cruelty as well as creatively exposing the ideas he was seeking to develop. Huxley's fiction was idea- rather than character- or plot-led. In *Point Counter Point* he has his first and wittiest success, though the central message is one of nihilism: 'Because that's what life finally is – hateful and boring,'[47] says Spandrell, a major character. In this attitude, Huxley was moving towards his next novel, *Brave New World*.

* * *

Huxley was still experiencing conflicting feelings about London and France: increasingly active in the peace movement that was beginning to flourish in Britain as the Continental political situation grew more seriously threatening, Huxley felt he needed to spend time in London. They took a flat in the Albany in Piccadilly, which gave Huxley access to the libraries and meetings he was missing. Self-consciously, they did not furnish it as a home; that was still in Sanary.

After the success of *Brave New World*, writing his next novel, *Eyeless in Gaza*, was more difficult. Huxley was still battling out the perennial conflict between his moral and aesthetic sides: on the one hand, he believed strongly in democracy and mass participation; on the other, he was repelled by crowds and offended by an invasion of privacy.

> It's sad that all the things one believes in – such as democracy, economic equality etc – shd *[sic]* turn out in practice to be so repulsively unpleasant – hot, smelly crowds; banana skins; building estates like skin eruptions on the landscape; loud speakers and gramophones every ten yards; roads made nightmarish with rushing traffic.
>
> Letter to Mary Hutchinson, 14 August 1934[48]

Unable to write and suffering from insomnia and ill health, the Huxleys came back to Sanary in summer 1934. He was overwhelmed by the beauty:

Such flowers and greenery I never saw here. I have been
doing rather little – lying rather fallow, as I don't seem able
to get what I want in my projected novel.

Letter to Mary Hutchinson, 19 May 1934[49]

Maria, too, revelled in the sunshine and beauty:

You have never been here when the cumulative madness of
five months of sun and country and stars make the world
unreal in its pleasures and beauties – and when the northern
sobriety is very northern and unreal indeed. I shall be so
sensible this winter *but I am so happy now*.

Letter to Eddy Sackville-West, June 1934

Huxley finally finished *Eyeless in Gaza*, which was published in
1936 just as Europe was beginning to crumble under fascism;
war threatened, and though he was heavily involved with the
peace movement, it did little to soothe his sense of foreboding. In
a letter to a friend, Maria expressed her fears that he had decided
to sell the house in France and that their days on the Riviera were
numbered. She was right: that summer was their last.

In the bleak winter of 1937, they went to Sanary for the
last time to clear the house, burning great bundles of manuscripts and giving away books and other belongings. The threat
of war was the main reason for the Huxleys' decision to leave
Europe for America. There was also Huxley's constant low-level
'illness', which kept him to his bed and meant he could not

write, their plans for Matthew's further education and Huxley's eternal restlessness.

Sad at the thought of leaving their beloved Mediterranean – which, Maria said, was 'irreplaceable in my heart' (letter to Mary Hutchinson, 1937) – they sailed in April on the SS *Normandie* for New York.

America – especially California, where they settled – was good for them. Huxley mellowed and indeed by the time the war ended he was being seen in quite a different light. Cyril Connolly, interviewing Huxley for *Picture Post*, wrote of him as a sort of saintly figure:

> If one looks at his face one gets first an impression of immense intelligence, but this is not unusual among artists. What is much more remarkable and almost peculiar to him is the radiance of serenity and loving-kindness on his features; one no longer feels 'what a clever man' but 'what a good man', a man at peace with himself and plunged as well – indeed, fully engaged – in the eternal conflict between good and evil, awareness and stupidity.[50]

Maria died in 1955 and Huxley's second wife, Laura, spoke of him after his death in 1963:

> I cannot tell you how gentle and tender the man was: accepting and tender and caring.[51]

Leonard Woolf spoke of his:

Essential gentleness and sweetness.[52]

Of the two sides of the man, the anger seems to have subsided as he grew older. Prophetically, his mother, who was an exceptional teacher and judge of character, had written him a deathbed exhortation:

Judge not too much and love more.

He had kept it all his life.

EPILOGUE

In his literary guide to the French Riviera (2004), Ted Jones wrote:

> Writers created the legend of the Côte d'Azur, and, down the ages, writers have perpetuated it.[53]

This was the starting point for my journey through the lives of six writers who lived on the Riviera. Through them, I hoped to deepen my understanding of the place and come to terms with it – its beauty, but also its vulgarity; its perfection, but at the same time the hollowness it hides. Although they did not write about their surroundings in their fiction, which was set elsewhere, they did write about it in their letters and diaries, where they marvelled at its beauty and magic.

For them all, it was a special, enchanted place where they found the physical and emotional peace to write some of their best works. The inspiration of the location affected them in different ways. Katherine Mansfield felt it was the similarities she found with New Zealand that woke her memories of child-hood and allowed her to relive her youth in *Prelude*.

> For one thing and it's awfully important the sea is here −
> very clear and very blue. The sound of it after such a long
> silence is almost unbearable − a sweet agony, you know −
> like moonlight is sometimes. And then there are the high
> mountains covered with bright green pine trees. Tufts of
> rosemary grow among the rocks and a tall flower with pink
> bells which is very lovely.
>
> Journal, 28 November 1915

For Wharton, it was the perfect natural beauty that was so over-whelming, it was spiritually fulfilling:

> …the heavenly beauty & the heavenly quiet enfold me, & I
> feel that this really is the Cielo della Quieta to which the soul
> aspires after its stormy voyage.
>
> Letter to Bernard Berenson, December 1920

The effect of this beauty was to inspire a rush of creativity. Mansfield described it in spring-like terms in a Christmas letter to Middleton Murry:

> I feel now that I only have to get into the sun and I'll simply
> burst into leaf and flower again.
>
> Letter to Murry, 23 December 1917

138

Wharton used very similar imagery in her novel *Summer*:

> The only reality was the wondrous unfolding of her new self,
> the reaching out to the light of all her contracted tendrils.
> She had lived all her life among people whose sensibilities
> seemed to have withered for lack of use.[54]

However, *Summer*, like Mansfield's *Prelude*, was not set on the Riviera but much closer to the writer's earlier home in West Massachusetts. Just as the South of France gave Maugham the strength, the peace and the inspiration to write his very English masterpiece *Cakes and Ale*, it provided Wharton and Mansfield with the emotional context they needed to imagine and relive their pasts. Wharton's Pulitzer Prize-winning novel, *The Age of Innocence*, was also partly written in Hyères but set in childhood New York.

For Huxley, too, the South of France provided the ingredients he needed for his best-known and most influential novel, *Brave New World*. Just as for the others, the distance from home gave him the perspective to see it clearly – in his case, not as it had been but as it could be.

For them all, the Côte d'Azur was a space rather than a setting, a gap in which they could do some of their most intense work. Freed from the day-to-day responsibilities and social obligations of home, the writers could indulge their imaginations in ways they might not have ventured before. Professionally, too, they were able to live comfortably without having to rely on earnings from journalism, which often distracted them from their creative work. Without social and financial pressure, surrounded by sunshine and beauty, they found the space, time and calm in which to write not what they saw but what they imagined.

The writers were solitary, and needed to be. Cocteau, sitting for days, alone, in front of the mirror in his hotel room, was self-consciously aware that he was an image of all creation – asking himself repeatedly, 'What am I?' From his isolation and self-reflection (he was aware of the punning), he rebuilt himself as an artist and a writer. Similarly, though less dramatically, the other writers removed themselves, cut themselves off even from their own language (only Maugham and Wharton were really fluent in French), which for communicators is a radical act, in order to force themselves inwards to find and tap the world of their imaginations. That they were successful is clear in terms of what they wrote, for they all created their masterpieces in the South of France: *Prelude*, *Cakes and Ale*, *The Age of Innocence*, *Tender is the Night* and *Brave New World* are still among the most important novels of the twentieth century, while Cocteau's creations of mixed media ballet, film and oratorios were some of the lasting foundations of art in the last century.

And yet there was a downside to this exile and isolation, one that can be seen even in the titles of the writers' works, which are quotations from, and references to, the masters: Shakespeare, Keats, Wordsworth and the painter Joshua Reynolds are referenced, as well as the ancient Classics. One senses the writers are identifying with the long tradition to which they belong to compensate for feelings of isolation and foreignness.

The price of solitude was loneliness. As people of letters, the writers missed libraries and (English) books and yearned for like-minded people and their friends. Keeping the healthy balance between solitude and socialising was problematic. Although the peace and quiet was essential for their work, it came at a high price. Mansfield's letters to John Middleton Murry include as many requests for the latest books from London as for him to come down to be with her. Maugham and Huxley went to London once or twice a year to meet their publishers and to stock up on books, toiletries (for Maugham) and London gossip.

Unlike the artists, who formed collectives, the writers were not a group and indeed sought to avoid each other as much as possible, though they were friendly with other creative people, such as painters, composers and dancers, and with politicians. Although Maugham generously invited fellow writers to his palatial home, they came as disciples, sitting at the feet of the Master, rather than equals. In the main, other writers were seen as rivals or distractions, and when eminent German authors fleeing Nazi Germany arrived in Sanary-sur-Mer, Huxley was dismayed rather than welcoming.

Instead of mixing with each other, the writers preferred to import their own guests to stay. In this way, they could structure the socialising around their own need for time alone in which to write. Wharton and Maugham, with generous means and large houses equipped with staff, were famous for their house parties, but both kept up the discipline of morning writing, not meeting the guests until lunchtime. The Huxleys were equally hospitable but of more limited means, and in their case it was Maria, Aldous' wife, who entertained the guests in the mornings while Aldous wrote. All the writers managed to discipline themselves to concentrate on their writing, but it was not only other people who were distracting: there were other inner demons too.

For Fitzgerald and Cocteau, drink and drugs were constant temptations: the need to avoid them had brought Fitzgerald to France in the first place. But it was not only substances that they found abusive: for both men, the very presence of friends and company acted as a stimulant, leading them to exhibitionism and a desire to dominate the party and become the focus of everyone's attention. Shocking other guests, offending their hosts and misbehaving were regular features of evenings with both men, and ultimately they became self-destructive. Fitzgerald's wife, Zelda, who encouraged his urges, was also destroyed by them, with a dire effect on her mental health. Foreshadowed in *Tender is the Night*, Fitzgerald sought to face and control these demons in his writing and out of that misery created his great work.

For Mansfield and for Huxley, the demons were physical: Mansfield was dying from TB and, in all likelihood, also from gonorrhoea. Coughing blood, weak and in pain, there were days when she could almost reach out to touch death, it felt so close; but others when the world was so warm and so beautiful she could believe in immortality. This is the essence of the world she recreated in *Prelude*, an intense love letter to the ephemeral beauty of youth and the world. For Huxley, who had already suffered a traumatic period of blindness as a teenager, recurring weakening of sight had been one of the reasons for coming into the bright light of southern France. Throughout his time at Sanary, he carefully rationed the use of his eyes, reserved reading for important texts and did not waste the precious capacity if he could avoid it. Maria typed all his manuscripts and wrote many of his letters, while Huxley suffered every day the knowledge that he could, once again, be struck into darkness, a darkness he transposed into the vision of *Brave New World*.

For Maugham, as for Wharton, the South of France became a home; both had houses and lived there permanently, rather than being visitors. The more relaxed social norms of France made it an attractive alternative to home. In Maugham's case his sexuality and in Wharton's her divorce were a source of potential social embarrassment, if not criminal prosecution. They had both spent time as children in France and shared a schizophrenic sense of identity that led them to feel like outsiders in their home country. Wharton's and Maugham's success as novelists came in the same way: shy, lacking in self-confidence (Maugham stammered) and feeling that they did not belong, they created new worlds of the imagination from which they could not be excluded.

The six writers' lives coincided with the interwar years and the enormous social upheavals leading to the Second World War. The Huxleys left Europe because they could see the rise of fascism. Fitzgerald had gone home with Zelda, whose illness had grown so severe she was to remain in a mental hospital for the rest of her life. Mansfield was long dead and Wharton had died recently. Only Maugham and Cocteau remained and came back when the war was over, to find that so much had changed for ever.

Only the bleached bones of their passing remain to greet visitors to their homes: Mansfield's studio is returned to a shed; the gates of Maugham's mansion still stand but the plot has been built on and there are many more houses than when he held court here. Cocteau's sleazy Hôtel Welcome has become a smart boutique venue for touring American visitors with oversized suitcases, and Fitzgerald's house in Juan-les-Pins is the Hôtel Belles Rives. Standing outside in the semi-dark of the pine trees, I think of Mansfield's 'Honeymoon' short story and the intense bitter-sweetness she evoked. That is, after all, all that I need.

In the main, their houses do not tell their stories. Wharton, who was an authority on houses, wrote that a woman is like 'a great house full of rooms' where 'in the innermost room, the soul sits alone and waits for a footstep that never comes'.[55]

This painfully sad metaphor suggests that perhaps the elaborate homes of Wharton and Maugham were in reality carapaces within which they could hide themselves, half hoping to be discovered and half dreading it. What appeared to be show was perhaps the opposite.

If that is so, what is it we hope to find when we track down the homes and houses of our writers? Is it some remains that linger in the fabric and that we can somehow rub against? Or are we paying a visit out of our respect for the writer? Whatever the reason, the effect is nearly always disappointing and the house strangely insignificant compared with the author's work. In the very act of being open to the public, the house has lost its charm of discovery. We are better, I believe, with those houses that are in ruins or have been pulled down. Then we can rely on our imaginations, which are always more vivid, more beautiful and more inspired with our writers' works.

NOTES

———

1   Ted Morgan, *Somerset Maugham*, London 1980, p. 311

2   Katherine Mansfield, 'Honeymoon' (1923), in *Short Stories*, London 1986, p. 267

3   *Women in Love*, chapter 30, London 1920

4   Claire Tomalin, *Katherine Mansfield: A Secret Life*, London 1987

5   John Keats, 'Ode to a Nightingale', 1813

6   Katherine Mansfield, 'The Man Without a Temperament', 1920

7   Ibid.

8   Edith Wharton, *A Backward Glance*, New York 1934, p. 145

9   Review in *Excelsior* (11 May 1917) and then used in programme notes

10 Quoted in Frederick Brown, *An Impersonation of Angels: A Biography of Jean Cocteau*, London 1969, p. 251

11 'Jeu Royal', in *Plain-Chant*, Paris 1923

12 Brown, *An Impersonation of Angels*, p. 252

13 'Portraits-souvenir' (1931), in *Oeuvres Complètes* X, p. 84

14 Edith Wharton, *The Reckoning* (1902), in *The Descent of Man and Other Stories*, New York 1904

15 *Love Diary*, 31 May 1908

16 Edith Wharton, *Summer* (1917), Signet Classics edition, New York 1993, p. 27

17 Mrs Winthrop [Margaret] Chanler, *Autumn in the Valley*, New York 1936

18 Edith Wharton, *New Year's Day*, New York 1924

19 Godfrey Winn, *The Infirm Glory*, London 1967

20 W. Somerset Maugham, *The Summing Up*, London 1938

21 Ibid.

22 Ibid.

23 Ibid.

24 Elinor Mordaunt ['A Riposte'], *Gin and Bitters*, New York 1931

25 W. Somerset Maugham, *A Writer's Notebook*, London 1951, p. 194

26 Ibid.

27 F. Scott Fitzgerald, 'How to Live on Practically Nothing a Year',
    Saturday Evening Post, September 1924
28 F. Scott Fitzgerald, *Tender is the Night*, London 1959, p. 18
29 Ibid.
30 Ibid., p. 19
31 Ibid., p. 23
32 Ibid., p. 29
33 F. Scott Fitzgerald, entry in his ledger, autumn 1925
34 Ibid.
35 Ibid.
36 Fitzgerald, *Tender is the Night*, book 1, chapter 7
37 Ibid.
38 Ibid.
39 Sybille Bedford, *Jigsaw*, London 1989
40 Ibid.
41 Aldous Huxley, *Music at Night* (1931), quoted in Sybille Bedford, *Aldous
    Huxley: A Biography*, Vol. 1, London 1973, p. 239
42 Bedford, *Aldous Huxley*, p. 283
43 *Nash's and Pall Mall Magazine*, 1930
44 'The Despair of Aldous Huxley', interview in *Harper's* magazine, June
    1930
45 Aldous Huxley on François Leclerc du Tremblay losing his father at the
    age of ten in *Grey Eminence*, London 1941
46 Aldous Huxley, *Crome Yellow* (1921), London 2004
47 Aldous Huxley, *Point Counter Point* (1928), London 2018, p. 288
48 Quoted in Nicholas Murray, *Aldous Huxley: An English Intellectual*,
    London 2002
49 Ibid.
50 Cyril Connolly, *Picture Post*, 6 November 1948
51 Murray, *Aldous Huxley*
52 Julian Huxley (ed.), *Aldous Huxley: A Memorial Volume*, London 1966
53 Ted Jones, *The French Riviera: A Literary Guide for Travellers*, London 2004
54 Wharton, *Summer*, p. 33
55 Edith Wharton, *The Fulness of Life* (1893), in *Collected Stories*, New York
    2002

INDEX